SCHOOL WRITING

Open University Press

English, Language, and Education series

General Editor: Anthony Adams
Lecturer in Education, University of Cambridge

TITLES IN THE SERIES

SCHOOL WRITING

Discovering the ground rules

**Yanina Sheeran and
Douglas Barnes**

Open University Press
Milton Keynes · Philadelphia

Open University Press
Celtic Court
22 Ballmoor
Buckingham
MK18 1XW

and
1900 Frost Road, Suite 101
Bristol, PA 19007, USA

First Published 1991

British Library Cataloguing in Publication Data
Sheeran, Yanina
  School writing: discovering the ground rules. – (English,
  language, and education series)
  1. Secondary schools. Curriculum subjects. English
  language. Writing skills. Teaching
  I. Title   II. Barnes, Douglas   III. Series
  808.042071

  ISBN 0-335-09453-8

Library of Congress Cataloging-in-Publication Data
Sheeran, Yanina, 1949–
    School writing: discovering the ground rules/by Yanina Sheeran and
    Douglas Barnes.
        p.   cm.—(English, language, and education series)
    Includes bibliographical references (p.   ) and index.
    ISBN 0–335–09453–8
    1. English language—Composition and exercises—Study and teaching
  I. Barnes, Douglas R.   II. Title.   III. Series.
  LB1631.S489   1990
  808′.042′0712—dc20   90–20912
                                                                  CIP

Typeset by Scarborough Typesetting Services
Printed in Great Britain by St Edmundsbury Press Limited
Bury St Edmunds, Suffolk

Contents

General editor's introduction

Douglas Barnes requires little introduction to likely readers of this book. He was a key contributor to the pioneering *Language, the Learner and the School*, which has informed and inspired several generations of new teachers in its penetrating analysis of the nature of classroom dialogue. It was one of the first of a series of books to draw our attention to the significant responsibility of the school for Language across the curriculum, perhaps better expressed these days as 'whole school language policies'.

It is a pleasure, therefore, to welcome a new book by Douglas Barnes and his collaborator, Yanina Sheeran, now a lecturer and previously head of a comprehensive school humanities department. Together they have written a book that continues in the tradition begun by Barnes' earlier work. The present volume considers the processes of writing in school, again across some of the major subjects in the curriculum, notably science, the humanities and English. As the National Curriculum is being phased in throughout England and Wales, attention will need to be paid to the profile component of writing, and not by any means in English classes alone. Indeed, if the National Curriculum is to be delivered, it will be ever more necessary to revive the concept of language across (or perhaps better 'throughout') the whole curriculum. This book provides many sound suggestions for ways in which this may be done.

It belongs, at least in part, to a tradition of thinking about classrooms that was pioneered through the concept of alternative frameworks in science. There are many ways in which classroom dialogue, in speech or writing, differs from that of life outside school; there are 'ground rules' that need to be learned if the student is to make progress in terms of what is understood and intended by the teacher. A good part of this book explores these ground rules both in general and in particular subject areas. In doing so, it exposes some of the misunderstandings that may be set up and inhibit the processes of learning. As the authors point out: 'these tacit expectations or ground rules are seldom discussed with pupils, as the teachers themselves are largely unaware of them'. School learning, and especially learning through writing, is a particular kind of technical use of language, a register of its own, and teachers need to be aware of the problems that may be created for their pupils if they are insufficiently inducted into this process.

In brief, this is what the book is about. It is based upon a wide variety of observations of classrooms in action and the frequent concrete references to particular lessons give an immediate feel of authenticity to the work. It is important to read the book as a whole and not just those chapters that apply to one's own particular subject. Part of the pupils' difficulty may be the lack of connection between the standards and expectations in different subject areas. One strength of *Language, the Learner and the School* was the eclectic range of subjects from which its examples were drawn. The present volume shares that strength. Now that we are much more conscious of the need for whole school policies, and school-based in-service days are commonplace, a book such as this could serve as a text through which whole schools could analyse their policies and improve their practices. Apart from the penetrating analysis of much current practice that it provides, the book is copiously supplied with suggestions for ways in which teachers can improve what takes place in the writing classroom.

Several other books in this series have looked from a variety of perspectives at the writing process at different ages. The unique feature of the present volume is that it explores this issue from the standpoint of what is taken as knowledge within secondary school subjects. In doing so, it adds a philosophical element to what is generally perceived mainly in psychological terms. It thus takes us beyond the concerns of the writing process alone to engage with more fundamental questions about how pupils make meanings for themselves and the role played by writing in their engagement with ideas. This can be seen, for example, in Chapter 2 in the discussion of scientific writing and in the illuminating discussion of the controversy between Britton and Williams about the nature of writing in a public domain – 'an established set of rules and practices, with a distinctive philosophical base'. Sheeran and Barnes provide here a clearly argued and balanced consideration of the issues involved. The book should be read especially for what it has to say about subjects other than those which we teach: English teachers can learn from what is said about writing in science, and vice versa. It distils the wisdom of much sensitive classroom observation by its two authors and encourages the reader to engage in a professional dialogue also.

The debate about classroom language has been with us for several decades; the present volume is a distinguished contribution that carries the debate into new and illuminating territory.

Anthony Adams

Preface

This book is written with both teachers and pupils in mind. It is the outcome of our desire to understand more clearly the processes involved in children's thinking and writing in secondary schools. We hope that it sheds some light on the reasons for some of the difficulties faced by pupils, and encourages teachers to experiment with new techniques to enhance their chances of success. Above all, we hope that the ideas we have put forward will enable teachers to empathize with the situation of learners, as we believe that is an essential prerequisite for effective communication in the classroom.

Our findings and recommendations are based largely on a study of science and humanities teachers and pupils that involved the use of questionnaires and informal interviews, as well as the observation of lessons and the collection of samples of written work. Material is also drawn from action research work conducted as a part of normal teaching, and in addition we have used material from several studies of English teaching.

Acknowledgements

We would like to thank the many teachers and pupils who have cooperated with us in the research for this book. Also our thanks go to Neil Mercer and Derek Edwards for exploratory discussions about ground rules.

1 Introduction

Discovering the ground rules of schooling

Teachers in secondary schools often find that pupils who have joined successfully in the discussion in a lesson, showing every sign of understanding, later hand in written work that is quite inadequate. That is the starting point for this book, to inquire why this should be and what might be done about it. It would be easy to dismiss these pupils as idle, but this is often manifestly untrue. In this chapter we offer some suggestions about the difficulties for pupils presented by writing in school subjects, and then go on in later chapters to consider writing in science, the humanities and English.

Those of us who learnt to write fluently and easily in our primary schools often forget what a complex set of competences are involved even in the simplest-seeming act of communication. We assume too easily that a task that is straightforward to us is equally unambiguous to pupils, forgetting that there was a time when we too had to learn the unspoken rules. This book is about learning unspoken rules: here we call them 'ground rules', though some of the ideas suggested by 'rules' are not appropriate. Much of the book will be dedicated to exploring the functions of ground rules in written work in secondary schools.

Part of the essential equipment of a teacher is an understanding of the nature and source of the difficulties experienced by pupils. Classroom communication shares the uncertainty of all talk, formal or informal: teachers find it as hard to understand pupils as pupils to understand teachers. Part of pupils' difficulties arise, of course, from the fact that they are being offered unfamiliar ways of looking at the world, but there are also difficulties of other kinds. In order to show themselves to be 'good pupils' and 'intelligent', children have to perform acceptably in contexts that are controlled by teachers. (In fact, they are only partly controlled, because most teachers inherit their classroom practices and expectations from their predecessors rather than invent them anew.) In the classroom, teachers operate complex systems of tacit expectations and norms, which deeply influence how they interpret their pupils' behaviour. There is nothing sinister in this: we all organize our behaviour in familiar social contexts by such tacit expectations. Education, however, is suffused with evaluative procedures: grading and selection are among its central functions, both through formal testing and through the everyday acceptance or rejection of pupils' contributions. For this reason, the teachers' tacit expectations are of urgent importance to pupils, as they define the conditions that the pupils must meet in order to display competence as learners and achieve success in school.

In spite of their importance, these tacit expectations or ground rules are seldom discussed with pupils, because the teachers themselves are largely unaware of them. The teachers' taken-for-granted beliefs about how the world of school is, and how teachers and pupils should behave, will have been learnt unconsciously during their own schooling and during their probationary years as teachers so that they do not find it easy to reflect on the ground rules that they are operating. Ground rules of different kinds relate to various aspects of classroom life. For example, teachers expect children to know what is relevant both when they offer contributions to lessons and in their writing. They expect them to adopt particular modes of thought, some of them very unlike the way people think and solve problems in everyday life. Indeed, some important ground rules relate to how children's knowledge from outside school is to be used or ignored during lessons. Teachers also have requirements about appropriate styles of talking and writing, and in some cases these requirements may be made explicit to the pupils – at least in part, as we shall see. Some of these different kinds of ground rules are illustrated in the pages that follow.

We begin with a frivolous example of the tacit meanings that shape a teacher's expectations.

> *Maths teacher:* What do you get if you cut a potato in half, then in half again, and then in half again?
> *Sharon:* Chips, sir.

The joke depends precisely upon the different ground rules operated at that moment by the teacher and by Sharon. The teacher's attention is focused upon the mathematics of halving; for him 'potato' is no more than a gesture towards the real world. The word directs Sharon's attention, however, towards occasions when she has cut up potatoes for a real purpose.

Similar to this is an example given by Edwards and Mercer (1987), whose book *Common Knowledge* contains a discussion of ground rules to which we ourselves are considerably indebted. They introduce the idea of 'the ground rules of educational discourse' with a question remembered from a secondary maths class from years before. (The reader may care to attempt to answer it.)

> Suppose you are the conductor of a bus. The bus leaves the depot on the way to the town centre. At the first stop it picks up 12 people. At the next stop another 11 get on. At the third stop 7 get off and 15 get on. At the fourth stop 21 people get off and

14 get on. The bus continues to the next stop where 7 people get off and a drunk climbs aboard. The conductor takes his fare, but the drunk is disruptive, and at the next stop 13 people complain to the conductor, and get off the bus. The conductor tells the drunk to get off. The drunk does so reluctantly, after first asking the conductor's name.

The teacher's questions were:
1 How many passengers are still on the bus?
2 What is the conductor's name?

This joke works in a way similar to the other one. We adults have been socialized into the ground rules of maths problems and know that the introductory sentence 'Suppose you are the conductor of a bus' can safely be ignored, because it is clearly the figures that matter. For this reason, most adults cannot answer the second question until they look back at the whole message. That is, one of the ground rules that we learn might be formulated as: 'When attempting a mathematical problem attend only to the numerical data and their interrelationships, and not to the contextual details.' A young child not yet socialized into these ground rules may actually find the second question easier to answer than an adult does.

The point of quoting these jokes is to demonstrate that we do learn to operate ground rules about what is relevant to maths problems and what can be ignored, and that these rules, though they guided our actions when we were pupils, are not necessarily available to our conscious inspection. Similar ground rules affect our reading of school tasks in all areas of the curriculum. We can ask ourselves: What are the ground rules about what constitutes 'reading' in school? (How, for example, is one expected to 'read aloud' to the teacher? In silent reading does one have to maintain the same speed as all the other pupils so as not to get ahead?) What constitutes an acceptable 'report' on a piece of practical work in science? What can be handed in as the outcome of a GCSE project in geography, and what cannot? What can an English 'composition' be, and what must it not be? In English too, unspoken ground rules define both what should be written and how it should be written.

Thus, whenever a teacher sets a writing task, the pupils' success depends upon their sharing that particular teacher's unspoken expectations about what will constitute an acceptable piece. Most teachers are to some degree aware of this, but very often the aspects of the written work that are most salient to them and their pupils are the written conventions. Several years ago, as part of a study of English teaching in the latter years of secondary schooling (Barnes *et al.*, 1984), a sample of 157 fifteen-year-olds was asked what they would have to change to improve their written work. Nearly half of their replies referred to spelling, punctuation or handwriting, many of them not mentioning the organization of ideas and the style of writing. Thus, whatever teachers intend to convey, in practice their pupils often 'hear' that surface conventions are the most important aspect of writing.

This is not to say that no teachers are concerned to communicate what they want. We shall show in Chapter 2 that many science teachers take pains to persuade pupils to write reports using a traditional format (Aim, Method, Result, Conclusion) and to adopt the passive voice ('The liquid was then heated . . .') in order to remove from the account any mention of the person who carried out the actions. It is our contention that even science teachers, and certainly teachers of other subjects, have requirements beyond these that they do not make so clear to their pupils, mainly because they are not themselves aware that there might be any difficulty. The problems that pupils face are very diverse and many of them are specific either to the subject matter being written about or to a particular teacher's expectations. Part of our intention in this book is to urge teachers to think more precisely about the nature of the tasks they set, and to discuss these with their pupils. Some of the difficulties their pupils face are created there and then in the classroom.

What ground rules apply to

Relevance

Let us begin with relevance. What is relevant to a lesson may be obvious to the teacher but not obvious to the pupils, who will not yet have mastered the principles by which their teachers judge whether a contribution is or is not related to the matter in hand. When a pupil writes a report on a demonstration in the chemistry laboratory, it is clear that the colour of the teacher's clothes is irrelevant, but it is harder to determine whether the colour of the chemical is equally irrelevant. It depends on what theoretical issue is in question, and whether the colour can be used to throw light upon it. One teacher interrupted his presentation with an urgent recommendation never to taste unknown chemicals, and thereby faced his pupils with a problem when they reported on the lesson for homework. The teacher's manner showed that it was a matter of acute importance, so some pupils gave it a major place in their report. Again, pupils may be uncertain whether to include in an account the shape of a flask or other piece of equipment, when it may be that this can only be decided in the light of a wider understanding of the matter in hand than they have at that moment. The ability to grasp many of these relevances thus rests upon the learner's growing understanding of the principles of the subject in question. In general, it is seldom clear what information should be included in an account and what should be taken for granted. In everyday conversation, we decide what to include on the basis of what we think that the other person knows already, but this is not possible to school children who must usually assume that their audience, the teacher, already has all of the necessary information. We now turn to other ground rules that are less obviously related to the needs of a curricular subject.

Hypothetical thinking: The 'what if?' realm

We also expect pupils to adopt particular ways of thinking about the world. A biology teacher introduced his class to seven ways in which living things are different from non-living things, and at the end of the lesson asked the pupils to devise for homework seven tests that could be used to discover whether something was living or not. However, the 'something' that the teacher chose – perhaps in order to give the task a certain concreteness – was a bunch of keys that he pulled from his pocket. Most of the class made a reasonable attempt at the task but there was a group of pupils who hardly tried to produce any tests. When they were later asked why not, it became clear that they saw no point in the task: 'We already know that they aren't living', one of them said. At first glance it seems a perfectly sensible response, yet it shows that they had not yet grasped one of the most pervasive of the ground rules that underlie schooling. Much if not most of what goes on in schools is not intended to be part of the everyday world, and certainly not to influence what happens in it. School work exists rather in the realm of 'what if?', a kind of never-never land in which ideas can be tried out. It is not unreasonable for children to want their activities to have a direct and useful relevance to their present and future lives, but if they do not realize that school activities are often quite different they are unlikely to succeed. We suspect that there may be a number of pupils who go through school without ever understanding or accepting this.

Disembedded logic

The removal of much of what goes on in lessons into a 'what if?' realm sets the pupils a problem in deciding what knowledge should be used and what should not be used. When as pupils we met traditional mathematical problems involving men digging holes, we had learnt not to ask whether all of them were equally energetic in that activity, or whether more men might have got in one another's way. We recognized that in the 'what if?' realm we were dealing not with real human beings but with abstractions; our task was to follow through an abstract 'disembedded' logic, not to think as we would in the real world. Pupils are faced with similar problems, usually in a more subtle form, and these can be illustrated by a task that was given to adolescents during a psychological study of their ability to make judgements (Peel, 1971). They were given the following statement and then required to answer questions about it:

> Doctors have discovered that people who have a disease called scurvy have swollen gums and painful sores. You are not likely to catch this if you have plenty of fresh fruit and vegetables in your diet.

One of the questions that the adolescents were asked to evaluate (Yes/No/Can't say) was 'Can you be ill through eating too much fruit?' This faced the pupils with the problem of deciding which ground rules were currently operating. Of course, they knew that in everyday life you can be ill from eating too much fruit, yet one of the ground rules that pupils learn early in their school careers is that they are expected to work within the boundaries of a question, using the given information and no more. If they make this assumption, and respond solely in terms of the question, the answer would have to be 'Can't say', because the statement provided no evidence on the matter. On the other hand, if they used their 'real-life' experience, they would have to answer 'Yes'. Schooling often faces pupils with this dilemma, of deciding whether to treat a question as an exercise in disembedded logic, quite separate from everyday life, or whether to utilize their 'common sense' by embedding the question in their out-of-school knowledge. Ironically, pupils are likely to have difficulty with this dilemma in the later stages of their schooling as well as in the very early ones. Some teachers of older students in sixth forms can be heard to complain that their pupils 'don't use their common sense', that is, they don't test school ideas against everyday experience. What the teachers have not realized is that those pupils have learnt all too thoroughly the ground rule about disembedded logic in their early years of schooling. In some subjects it is only at an advanced stage that everyday knowledge is held to be relevant to learning. Schooling thus faces pupils with the dilemma of intuiting what ground rules are being operated by a teacher at any particular moment.

Everyday knowledge

The interaction of school and everyday knowledge faces pupils with other dilemmas. The analytical categories used in school subjects sometimes cut across and apparently negate the practical categories used by learners in their everyday lives. In some cases, the everyday categories may represent inferior and potentially misleading descriptions of the world and these we can ignore. On other occasions, however, the difference between the technical and the everyday categories is arbitrary, and represents different practices and different purposes that the categories serve in everyday and technical discourse, without one being intrinsically superior to the other. Munby and Russell (1983) mention a girl who insisted that 'People aren't animals'; in most of our daily activities, of course, the differences that distinguish people from animals are more important than those that unite them. Similarly, Keddie (1971) mentioned some pupils who rejected a social studies teacher's attempts to establish the 'nuclear/extended family' distinction because, as one of them said, 'We know about families; we live in them', and the distinction did not match that experience.

What is in question in cases like these is the pupils' willingness to shift temporarily to an unfamiliar category system and to try it out as a means of seeing the world in an alternative manner. This shifting to alternative frames of reference is an essential part of academic learning, especially in its later stages:

older pupils are faced with a sequence of alternative 'what if?' worlds and are expected to take on each of them at one time or another, working through its implications and possibilities. Not all pupils are ready to shift to an unfamiliar category system, which requires them for the moment to put aside the taken-for-granted 'frames' of their everyday lives, which may well seem much more important than what school offers. Their willingness to do this must depend upon whether they trust the school's implicit promise that one day these activities will make sense. This ability, or willingness, to shift temporarily to alternative bases for classification – alternative ways of seeing the world, that is – is not only very important in formal schooling, but may be essential to some aspects of life in an industrial society. Pupils who resist these shifts of conceptual frame are unlikely to succeed in school. In most school subjects they are required not only to exclude their everyday knowledge, but to detect at which moments such bracketing is required of them. Curricular subjects differ in the extent to which they make such demands of students: Bernstein (1971a) characterizes curricula in terms of levels of 'framing', that is, the extent to which each assigns validity to conceptual systems from everyday life. The ability to 'bracket' everyday experience when required seems very important to school success; it may not be equally available to children from different social backgrounds.

Other ground rules

It must be clear to the reader that we are using 'ground rules' to refer to a variety of tacit expectations that school pupils have to learn to deal with. There are certainly more than the four kinds we have so far illustrated. Russell (1982) for example, points out that sometimes in lessons children are uncertain whether they are being asked how things look to them or how they really are. The teacher may be asking for a description or an expression of opinion, but is met with silence because the pupils think that she wants an authoritative statement of verifiable truth. This appears to be another ground rule that requires children to judge what the teacher is expecting. In a similar way, pupils are sometimes unsure whether a teacher is wanting them simply to reproduce in writing what has been presented in a lesson, or whether they are to manipulate and reinterpret the material, or even to add to it from their own experience. Different teachers place greater or lesser value upon a pupil's contribution to the thinking.

We see no need to assume that there is a limited number of ground rules, or that it is possible to define each of them in a formal and exhaustive manner. Several of those we have already described overlap with one another. Some ground rules appear to be implicit in schooling as a whole, others form part of particular subjects as they are currently interpreted in the curriculum, while still others form part of specific school activities. There may even be some that are created by a particular teacher. What we are looking at are not clear-cut logical categories, but aspects of cultural performances in particular contexts. This implies that they are unclear, changeable, open to reinterpretation by different teachers, and in the longer term open to question and therefore to deliberate modification.

Ground rules for discourse

We turn now to a sub-category of ground rules, those which relate to the styles of language that pupils are expected to use in school, and particularly in written work. Some of the ground rules so far discussed – the 'what if?' mode, for example – while they can only be detected through what is said and written, can hardly be considered a matter of the genre or style of language required without extending those terms so far as almost to deprive them of meaning. In Australia, there has been in recent years considerable debate whether it is useful to talk of 'genres' of school discourse, and whether such genres should be taught to pupils. Frances Christie (1985) and others have urged the importance of ensuring that the genres needed for taking part in school activities are made available to all pupils, and in doing so have used arguments very similar to those that we are advancing in relation to the more inclusive idea of ground rules. Later in this chapter we discuss some implications of using terms such as discourse and genre.

Teachers are not always aware when they set written work that what appears to be a straightforward task may present difficulties to their pupils in choosing an appropriate style of writing. We can illustrate this from a biology lesson in which 15-year-olds of average ability watched a television programme that dealt with decay in teeth. The manner of the programme's presentation was persuasive, being clearly intended to influence the pupils' behaviour. After showing the film, the teacher led a discussion that focused on the biological issues raised, and then asked the class to write for homework about the topic discussed in the lesson. Neither the teacher nor the pupils were aware of the dilemma that faced them. The film, although it contained scientific content, spoke directly to the young people in the language of persuasion. The class, however, had learnt a quite different style for writing in science lessons, often including a compressed 'note form'. Were they to reflect the style of the film or conform to the usual norms of school science writing? This ambiguity set them a dilemma that few were mature enough to deal with. Here is what one pupil wrote:

> Regular visits to the dentist are essential. Do not eat sweets between meals. Foods such as raw carrots and cabbage are good for the teeth. Teeth must be brushed at least twice a day. Especially at night. Always use a good make of brush.

The uncertainty of this piece of writing is not untypical of what the whole class wrote. The writer is unsure whether she is reporting the information given in the film and the discussion, imitating the directly addressed persuasions of the presenter, or writing 'science notes'. The pupils brought to the task existing frames of expectations for scientific discourse but were inevitably influenced by the alternative discourse frame offered by the film. The teacher's only hope of obtaining effective writing would have been to propose an explicit audience and purpose for the writing, perhaps spending a few minutes discussing with the class what would be required. Indeed, much writing in secondary schools would be improved if such a discussion were undertaken by all teachers whenever they set written work.

Christie (1985) reports an almost identical confusion of styles when 6-year-olds were asked to write 'a story' about a science lesson on the hatching of eggs – such difficulties seem to occur in any age group. She represents this as a failure by the teacher to communicate to the young children that a particular genre was required, appropriate to the generalizing purposes of science. Our next example, though concerned with language, can hardly be treated as a matter of a definable genre. There appear to be more general linguistic ground rules that are not to be associated with a specific genre, and certainly not the genre of a subject area.

Some very general language demands of schooling can be illustrated from a small research study carried out by Hawkins, an associate of Bernstein. He asked children from different social class backgrounds to look at a sequence of cartoons and narrate to him the events pictured in them (Hawkins, 1969). He reported that whereas working-class children tended to use pronouns rather than nouns (e.g. 'He kicked it through there'), middle-class children described the events more explicitly through the use of nouns ('One of the boys kicked the ball through a window', perhaps). Rosen (1972) pointed out, however, that because the adult being addressed could see the pictures as the children talked about them, those children who pointed and used pronouns were on the face of it behaving more appropriately. What the other children had done was to internalize the ground rules that apply to verbal display in a school context, and to apply these rules rather than the normal ones for talking to someone about pictures. They had learnt that in school you are expected to make formal presentations at a high level of explicitness, and not talk to an adult as you might at home. To put it another way, what distinguished the two groups was not their linguistic resources but their interpretations of the situation, their awareness of what ground rules the adult present was applying to the situation. What was required was not a specific genre but a level of explicitness that might characterize many genres. Though this example refers to spoken language, similar tacit expectations govern written presentation. Differences of interpretation like this are perfectly normal between people outside school; what makes them important in school is their implication in the processes of assessment and categorization of the children.

Access to ground rules

We are using the term 'ground rules' to apply only to norms and expectations that are tacit, not spelt out between teachers and pupils in spite of their importance for school success. Various groups of pupils appear to have more or less ready access to them, as Hawkins' (1969) study implies. To recognize a shift of ground rules, pupils may have to respond to vague or highly ambiguous signals from a teacher, or in many cases to make a leap of intuition in the absence of any signal at all. For example, a teacher once asked her pupils what was the shape of sand dunes. There was a picture of dunes in their textbook, and therefore some of the pupils attempted to describe what they saw, but the teacher soon interrupted this by saying, 'They are a special shape', with a slight emphasis upon 'special'. Some of the pupils responded to this signal by offering technical terms instead of informal descriptions, thus earning the teacher's approval: others failed to recognize the signal, and continued to offer descriptions in a way that made them seem less intelligent than the others. We can expect ground rules to be very lightly signalled, but more often not signalled at all, as in the example from Hawkins (1969) when the children had to guess that a verbal display was expected. Miller and Parlett (1976) have shown that even college students vary greatly in their ability to make use of the cues that their lecturers let fall.

As well as recognizing the existence of ground rules, pupils have to assess the strength of the explicit requirements laid upon them, that is, whether the teacher's remarks are to be interpreted as advice, suggestions or injunctions. One of us led a class in discussing the changes that could be identified in their home town by comparing a present-day map with an older map of the town. For homework they were given a still earlier map and asked to write about the changes that had taken place between the dates of the two maps. One boy produced a lively description of a seventeenth-century house in the area, and when asked why he had done so replied cheerfully that he knew the teacher would be interested, as indeed she would have been in another context. The boy had interpreted as a suggestion what the teacher intended as an injunction, perhaps because he had brought another set of ground rules from another context. Pupils have to learn to interpret the strength of teachers' requirements, but this may well be hindered by the operation of tacit ground rules already learnt. This too can be illustrated from our experience. Teachers following an advanced course at a university are sometimes asked as an exercise to plan in a realistic fashion an evaluation of some part of their own school's curriculum. Each year one or two of the teachers write an academic essay, however strongly the nature of the task is emphasized, and this is probably because their grasp of the ground rule that university lecturers want essays complete with academic paraphernalia is so strong that it overrides the explicit instructions. [Similarly, Dixon (1988) reports an occasion when older school students, given questions intended to suggest ideas for a piece of writing, treated them as a set of questions to be answered separately and sequentially.] Students of all ages have to learn not only the ground rules but also the 'meta-rules' that govern when and how the ground rules are to be applied.

The language of specialist disciplines

Ground rules apply to written and spoken communication alike. Some are general and apply to many contexts and subjects, but there are also ground rules that govern discourse styles specific to particular school subjects, particularly in writing. The practice of confining scientific reportage to passive sentence constructions has already been mentioned, but there is far more to it than that. Take, for example, an experienced teacher of biology who accepts an 11-year-old pupil's use of the word 'windpipe' but asks the rest of the class for 'the other word for "windpipe" ' ('trachea'), later introducing the term 'bronchus'. For her, inducting her pupils into the discourse of her science was an essential part of her professional responsibilities. This raises an underlying question about learning in all subjects. Those students who are going to study biology, or physics, or mathematics, or geography, or literature at a higher level – perhaps towards a degree – will need to use the language forms expected of specialists. Does this mean that all the others, who form the greater majority, must also do so? Behind this question lies a dilemma: Can we understand and use the conceptual structures of a discipline without also mastering the expected mode of discourse, including the language forms associated with it? The answer is not a simple one.

Our whole curriculum implies that everyone needs to have a grasp of a range of ways of understanding the world in order to be able to participate fully as a citizen. Moreover, it is often argued that it is impossible to grasp the ways of understanding that constitute a subject without being able to join in the discourse of that subject. Terms such as 'genre' and 'discourse', however, are ambiguous. Do they refer to the patterns of language forms that are commonly used by specialists in a subject, that is, the grammatical forms and the vocabulary? Or do they rather refer to the conceptual frameworks that underlie the register, the 'ways of knowing' made possible by it. Christie (1985) seems to imply that they refer to both, as if they were inseparable:

> Schools are . . . responsible for teaching ways of meaning, ways of knowing, ways of working and ways of enquiring. . . . Those [pupils] who fail in schools are those who fail to master the genres of schooling: the ways of structuring and dealing with experience that schools value in various ways. Children who fail in schools are those who operate with ways of meaning different from those of schooling.

It is indeed true that schools set out to teach their pupils different ways of understanding the world about them, and that some of these ways of thinking are very closely linked with the discourse modes expected in different subjects. (These issues are discussed in the following chapters in relation to science and humanities.) However, in our view, ground rules are more arbitrary and less clearly defined than in Christie's account, and less closely associated with the pattern of language forms than her choice of the word 'genre' seems to imply. The central question is, do the cognitive strategies, the patterns of enquiry and explanation, the preferences, values and the rule-of-thumb ways of going about things that constitute a subject depend on using the particular technical language of the subject, or could the same thoughts be conveyed in other words? (The example of 'windpipe' as a substitute for 'trachea' may be a special case.) Or, to put it differently, in order to participate in discourse in the sense of a way of meaning and understanding, does one have to master discourse in the sense of conforming to particular linguistic patterns? The issue has been debated with some heat and is still not resolved.

During the 1970s, a movement called 'Language Across the Curriculum' gathered support not only from some teachers but more officially from the Bullock Committee, whose report *A Language for Life* (DES, 1975) recommended that all schools should have a language policy. Language Across the Curriculum was interpreted in many ways in different places. One emphasis that is very pertinent to our present purposes is the view that in putting ideas into words, either spoken or written, school pupils may actually be learning. The movement thus proposed that writing is potentially a means of learning and not just of rehearsing knowledge provided by a teacher or a textbook. The two of us who have written this book are committed to the view that when a pupil sits down to write after a history lesson or a piece of practical work in science, in the struggle to represent the new ideas and experiences on paper, he or she is reordering thought: clearly this is not a matter of accumulating new information, but of rearranging and reinterpreting what is already partly known. Behind it lies the belief that all learning requires to a greater or lesser degree the active reordering of thought by the learner. For example, to understand 'erosion', it is not enough merely to be able to give a definition: true understanding of such a concept must necessarily reorder the learner's perceptions, sometimes extensively, so that when he or she looks at a map or at the countryside itself its patterns take on different meanings from before. Such reordering does not happen in a flash, nor does it take place solely through writing or discussion. The proponents of Language Across the Curriculum would argue, however, that some of the processes by which pupils begin to modify their understanding (of the patterns of land forms, in this case) can take place when they write or talk about a new concept (such as erosion) that has been presented to them. It is important to include the word 'can' in the formulation, as not all kinds of writing and talk are equally useful for this purpose.

Much of the thinking of the Language Across the Curriculum movement derived from the work of James Britton (Britton *et al.*, 1975). In 1966, he and his colleagues set up a Writing Research Unit at the University of London Institute of Education. Britton's contention was that younger children make sense of their experience partly through what he called 'expressive' uses of language: these referred to a kind of talking to oneself, which since it is not primarily adjusted to the needs of a reader is often inexplicit. Expressive writing would be non-technical in language, informal in tone, probably inexplicit, and imbued throughout with the writer's feelings and attitudes, though not necessarily in a form that would make these available to a reader. As young people mature, he maintains, they become more able to write in ways that take account of the need of potential readers, and this leads to uses of written language that he calls 'poetic' and 'transactional'. Nevertheless, in his view, expressive uses of language continue to play an important part even in adult life in communication with intimates, and perhaps in talking through problems to ourselves. 'Transactional' language, on the other hand, is involved in the world's business, persuading, planning, explaining, negotiating and doing. The name 'poetic' is potentially misleading, as it refers to uses of language that stand back to observe and respond rather than setting about changing the world. Britton's distinction between 'expressive' uses and the other two is certainly valuable, for it is important to realize that our language is sometimes primarily focused upon ourselves and our needs, and sometimes upon the needs of an audience, real or imaginary. Teachers have taken over the terms 'poetic' and 'transactional', and have used them to refer to literary and non-literary writing, though this does not precisely match Britton's definition.

Underlying the work of the Writing Research Unit was the belief that when pupils are required to write like adult members of a school discipline, and to use conventional discourse modes, this often impedes them from using the writing to reshape their understanding. To put it in the project's terms, when young people are struggling with new ideas, they should be able to write first in an expressive mode, because they need to be addressing themselves to the ideas and not to an imaginary audience of scientists, historians or literary critics. The project members argued that to force children to write in a transactional mode before they had gone some way towards grasping how to use the new ideas would encourage them to spin a thread of technical phrases that had little or no relationship with their understanding of the matters they were writing about. This would not exclude teaching them later to write in specialist styles when they were more secure in the knowledge and procedures in question.

Critics of the Writing Research Unit's stance (Williams, 1977; Richards, 1978) argue that the mode of understanding of a subject is inextricable from its discourse: to learn to think like a physicist one has to learn to talk and write like one, because the conceptual structures that constitute physics exist only in the specialist discourse of physicists. Thus, if pupils are deprived of an opportunity of learning to use the discourses of the disciplines, they are thereby being deprived of access to important ways of understanding the world, and trapped in commonplace everyday conceptions of reality.

It is useful at this point to explain the position that we take up in relation to this debate, as much of the rest of the book depends on this. We accept the view, nowadays often called 'constructivism', that human beings learn by basing their actions upon hypothetical models of how the world is, and modifying these models in the light of how the actions turn out. This can most readily be recognized in the physical world; for example, children expect that as water is heated it will become hotter and hotter, and have to revise this view when they discover that at a certain point the temperature levels off. The same process happens in learning about the social world of people and their behaviour, though in a less clear-cut fashion: a young child may find it comfortable to approach teachers for a personal chat, and perhaps benefit from this until one teacher shows unmistakably that she does not see this as appropriate. Our constructions of how the world is are thus gradually modified, and we take an active part in this. The central point of the constructivist view is that experience and meaning does not come to us ready-made, we have to construct it for ourselves. This corresponds well with the Language Across the Curriculum movement's stress on the role of writing and talking as a way of learning, but does not necessarily commit us to sharing their view of the function of expressive uses of language in learning. That is discussed in Chapter 2.

It is useful at this point to consider the relevance of the views of the Writing Research Unit to ground rules. Their central concern was to argue that writing and talking in an informal manner helps the learner to relate new ideas, experiences and information to his or her existing pictures of the world. The corollary of this is that using the special discourse of a school subject should be postponed until the learner had made some progress towards grasping the conceptual framework of the subject. Taking over the discourse mode of an academic subject is more complex than at first appears. For example, it is far from being merely a matter of using a set of technical terms: in moving into a new discipline the learner is shifting his or her view of some aspect of the world. The technical vocabulary is useless unless it is the visible tip of a network of concepts that can be used to generate thinking in other contexts. Writing an acceptable piece is a matter of far more than just couching existing ideas in the wrappings of new words. Our argument in this book is that writing in school requires the writer to take over both new conceptual structures and (at the same time) to manage sets of ground rules, some general to school as a whole, some related to the curricular subject, and some specific to a particular occasion and teacher.

Ground rules in written work

What are the requirements of school writing tasks? Many teachers, well socialized into the ground rules of the writing that they themselves have to do, cannot understand why pupils have difficulty with school tasks. When we write we do not begin with a fully formed message, even when the overall thrust of what we want to say is clear: during writing we shape not only the words but the ideas they represent. If we are skilled writers, we are also responding to the supposed interests and needs of the audience we have in mind. Tortured and unclear prose is often a sign that in the struggle to shape the ideas the writer has not reached full control of the content he or she is writing about. But our contention is also that those pupils who write well, do so in part because they have succeeded in penetrating the unspoken ground rules operated by their teachers. Thus pupils are grappling with several simultaneous demands:

1 Trying to make sense of the subject matter and reorder it in a form that makes subjective sense.
2 Carrying out the teacher's explicit requirements for content, genre, style and lay-out.
3 Intuiting the unspoken requirements of the task (i.e. the ground rules).

Among the complexities must be included the fact that though the teacher may explicitly require, for example, an historical piece addressed to an imaginary Tudor audience, or a science report in the style of a scientific journal, the pupil is aware that the work will in fact be read by the teacher – and probably by the teacher alone – not for the purpose of gaining information but as a means of assessment. Thus there may be conflict between the explicit requirements and the ground rules.

Among the implications of this is that the teaching of writing is the business of all teachers: it cannot be left to English teachers alone. Writing is not a skill that can be practised in English lessons and then applied elsewhere. As the list above implies, each lesson faces the young writer with its unique problems. Clumsy and muddled writing may arise from the struggle to make sense of unfamiliar ideas, for most of us write best about familiar topics, and for this reason alone there would be good reason to offer pupils some help in ordering their writing. Our prime interest here, however, is the pupil's grasp of the teacher's expectations, both those that are explicit and those we are calling 'ground rules'. Thus, when we say that the teaching of writing is the business of all teachers, we are not referring to spelling and punctuation or to the ordering of content – though teachers may well interest themselves in these – but to helping pupils to consider what ground rules will be appropriate in a particular piece of writing. There is every reason to think that if the tacit requirements were habitually explored with pupils there would be a general improvement in written work. However, 'explored' here is not a euphemism for telling the pupils what is wanted. The teacher would need to find out what the pupils *thought* was required as a basis for understanding how to explain effectively; without an insight into the pupils' preconceptions, the teacher's explanations might prove unhelpful, as some of our examples show. In the final chapter, we develop further the idea that if teachers were to discuss ground rules with their pupils, an improvement in written work would be likely; in our view, there is much more to this than transmitting the unambiguous requirements of a genre.

Differences in access to ground rules

All children must learn to operate ground rules appropriately, but some are more successful at this than others. Those who fail may be seen by their teachers as unintelligent, ill-mannered or uncooperative. This may play a part in the disadvantage in schooling known to be experienced by many children from working-class families. However, our material will allow us only to speculate about this.

Our own experience as teachers leads us to think that children from middle-class, especially professional, homes find it easier to accept success in schooling as an end in itself, or at least as a route to qualifications. Working-class parents know that for some young people schooling is a way to advancement, but many have been led by past experience to exclude themselves and their children from this. Perhaps as a result, children from working-class homes are quicker to demand that what they learn in school has a visible relevance and usefulness in their present and future lives. This would be likely to make them less ready to take the 'what if?' mode seriously or to be willing to hold in suspense their own sense of how the world is. (A similar view has played its part in educational policy for many years, from the Newsom Report of 1963 to the Technical and Vocational Education Initiative of 1983.)

In surveying different kinds of ground rules, we have illustrated how pupils have to learn to operate in the 'what if?' realm, ignoring everyday knowledge and interpreting school tasks as requiring an abstract, disembedded logic unlike thinking in everyday life. Moreover, they are often expected in lessons to adopt alternative categories and explanatory frames that may negate those they take for granted in their lives outside school. We suggested that the ability to bracket everyday experience may not be equally available to children from different social backgrounds. In doing so, we mentioned Keddie's example of the pupils who rejected the concept of the nuclear family, but did not add that they were members of a bottom set or that Keddie used this and other material to argue that working-class children – the main inhabitants of bottom sets – experienced a different curriculum from pupils in top sets. Part of her argument was that pupils in top sets were more willing to take over school tasks and frames of reference uncritically, and that it was the children in bottom sets who challenged them. The concept of ground rules gives us a way of understanding why this should be.

However, this is not the only way in which pupils' social backgrounds might influence their school performance. Not all ground rules are signalled by means of identifiable cues; we illustrated this from Hawkins's study of children from different social class backgrounds telling a story based on a series of cartoons. The middle-class children were able to ignore the apparent demands of the situation – sharing a picture story with an attentive adult – and impose on it their tacit knowledge of the likely ground rules: they 'knew' that a particular kind of verbal display was required. Bourdieu (1974) has argued that middle-class children take to school a body of 'cultural capital' in the form of knowledge of the 'style' of behaviour that is required to meet school demands; working-class children, deprived of these cultural competences, are reduced to rote learning, since their attempts at more imaginative participation are rejected by teachers because they are inappropriate in 'style'. It is possible to interpret Bourdieu's ideas as an alternative way of approaching what we are calling 'ground rules', but with a very explicit reference to social class differences in school success.

In the late 1960s and early 1970s, much attention was attracted by Bernstein's hypothesis about the role of 'sociolinguistic codes' in school success. Partly because of Bernstein's own earlier characterization of these codes, they were often confused with superficial aspects of children's use of language, such as social class differences in accent and grammar. In Bernstein's later formulation of the hypothesis (Bernstein, 1971c), the codes referred to different linguistic usage, which reflected not different language resources but different ways of interpreting situations. Our argument is that we can understand some aspects of school failure better by seeing that all pupils have to gain access to ground rules than by positing the existence of two contrasting sociolinguistic codes. The matter is a great deal more complex than that. Indeed, the view that successful participation in schooling depends upon being able to use 'elaborated code' has itself been persuasively questioned by Cooper (1976).

The next chapter deals with ground rules for writing in science lessons and Chapter 3 with writing in the humanities. Chapter 4 discusses the different expectations that English teachers are likely to have for writing in their lessons. The final chapter offers to teachers some practical suggestions for ways of discussing ground rules with their pupils, and also considers some of the functions of subject genres and other kinds of ground rules both in school and in society as a whole.

2 Scientific language

For some years now, there has been a controversy about the kind of writing children should be doing in science lessons. Traditionally, most science teachers have expected children to use the impersonal and objective language of science reports. The model for this kind of language can be found in science textbooks, in the language of scientific journals and, usually, in the science teachers' own experience of schooling. But for about the past 20 years there has been a challenge to this convention. Writers like Britton *et al.* (1975) and others associated with the Language Across the Curriculum movement have argued that children need to use language in different and more informal ways in order to learn effectively and that a wider range of writing styles should be encouraged in science lessons. This view gained ground during the 1970s, especially with the official approval of the Bullock Report (DES, 1975). But it has also been heavily criticized, both by teachers in schools and by academics (e.g. Williams, 1977). Williams, for example, argues that thought and language are inextricably linked, and that children will not think 'scientifically' unless they use the language usually associated with the subject. Britton and his associates, on the other hand, consider that the use of subjective and informal language will actively assist children's learning.

In this chapter, we shall explore the main issues involved in this controversy, using the concept of 'educational ground rules' and 'framework theory' to enhance our understanding of some of the problems. The discussion is based largely on the careful examination of scripts produced by pupils and also on interviews with both pupils and teachers. For it is only by beginning with the views and concerns of science teachers and by looking at what pupils achieve and why, that we can come to conclusions that have real implications for classroom practice, in the sense that they are embedded in teachers' and pupils' daily experiences of teaching and learning. (Most teachers who read this will easily be able to find similar examples of their own, to compare with ours.) Then, having established a mass of evidence about what teachers want and what children write and why, the latter part of the chapter is devoted to a reappraisal of the academic debate concerning writing in science. Finally, the implications of all the findings are discussed, in relation to future classroom practice.

To begin, it is worth considering what is involved when children write in the accepted language of science. Figure 2.1 is a typical example of a traditional written account of an experiment conducted in a class of 13-year-old pupils. Readers might like to speculate about what a teacher can learn from such a piece of writing: what the pupil has understood; what you cannot tell from it; and how you follow it up in a subsequent lesson. Impersonal language and the use of a report format like the one illustrated are favoured by many science teachers for a number of reasons and, despite other changes in science pedagogy, remain predominant, especially in the later years of secondary schooling, even though they have been heavily criticized over the past two decades. We begin by examining the reasons for science teachers' loyalty to this kind of language.

First, it is traditional to write in this way in science lessons. It therefore presents itself to teachers as the 'obvious' kind of writing to set when teaching science and a familiar routine from their own schooldays, in most cases. One teacher we questioned could find little to justify the use of impersonal language except that it was accepted practice within the scientific community:

I: You've said that when pupils are writing up you prefer them to use this impersonal way of writing. I wonder if you have any particular reasons for doing that.

T: No, apart from it being accepted practice. Those who are going to go on further with science have to do it, I suppose, so . . .

There is an emphasis here on serving the needs of the small minority of pupils who will study the subject at an advanced level, in that this kind of writing is considered to be a necessary skill within the academic scientific community. By contrast, the teacher who disagreed most with explicitly teaching pupils to write in one rigid way showed more concern about the likely futures of those pupils who were not going to specialize in science:

. . . because based on the fact that 99% of them are not going to be sort of experimental scientists who are going to have to write papers you know. . . . I mean this is what the old-fashioned system seems to be producing, perhaps aiming at 'A' level and things like that which is rather stupid as people are not going to do that.

Traditional ways of doing things often exist because they are the tried and tested ways of doing things best but, equally, many traditional techniques are not the most effective way of achieving your desired objectives. Tradition by itself, therefore, is not a sufficient justification for the domination of a particular style of writing in science, and we must therefore look further for other reasons for demanding its use, if we are to achieve the aim of assessing the relative merits of the two positions we outlined at the start of this chapter.

Getting Copper From Copper Ore!

<u>Aim</u>:- TO get copper from a copper ore.

<u>Apparatus</u>:-

Bunsen, mate, wire gauzes, tripod Beakers (two) filter paper and Filter funnel.

<u>Method</u>:-

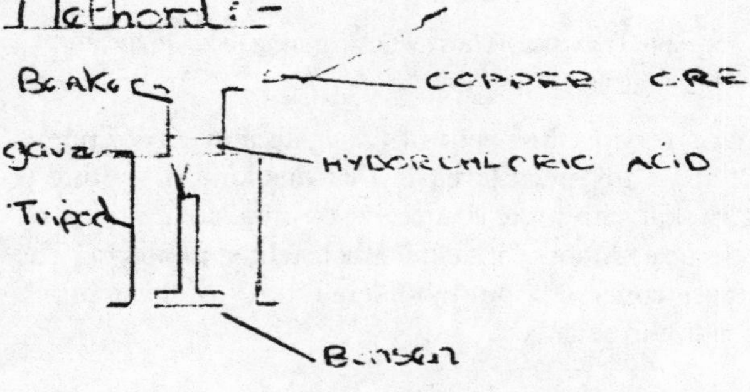

Copper ore is add to Hydrochloric aci and the water colour changed black, then green then grey. Then the mixture that was left in the Beaker got Filtered

Figure 2.1 Getting copper from copper ore
A typical example of traditional report writing in science

as shown below.

Filter
funel   Filter paper

                        Beaker

Then the beaker was set up like
this :

                    6v

Carbon electrodes   Copper Chloride
                                  Solution

With adding 6 volts to the copper chlorid
-e Solution, these was bits of copper
on the bottom.

Conclusion.

   It was found out that by heating,
filtering and (Electrofing) by usingElectric
you can get Copper from its ORE.

We can do this best by looking at some of the main characteristics of this kind of writing, then asking teachers why they consider those characteristics to be important. Then, by looking at the pupils' responses, we should be able to come to some assessment of the merits of the teachers' arguments.

The report format

The format of 'Aim, Method, Result, Conclusion' is the most immediately obvious feature of the example we have used. Teachers offered three major justifications for its use. Some of them explained to pupils that if anyone else wanted to check their experiments to test their validity, they would be able to do so because of the precision of the description given. Here is an example of such a justification from a science workbook designed for pupils by teachers:

> When you do a scientific experiment, it is important to write down all the details of what you are trying to find out, how you performed the experiment, what you discovered etc. . . . This is necessary so that if someone else or even you, wants to repeat it and check your findings or arguments, then they can do so . . .

Teachers who use this kind of justification are attempting to communicate to pupils some idea of the importance and universality of the scientific method, in a concrete enough way for all pupils to understand. And, of course, adopting the format of the scientific report is also a way of encouraging pupils to see themselves as apprentices to the scientific community, working according to the rules of scientific method. But the extract also gives another reason for the pupils to use this format, and that is that it will clarify their own thinking. This is probably a more important reason than the appeal to public accountability, because in the normal run of school science it is unlikely that anyone else except the teacher will ever check their experiments. After all, however much we may try to give pupils original tasks, most experiments conducted in science lessons are not novel ones at the leading edge of scientific discovery. Thus we need to look instead particularly closely at the justification that emphasizes the usefulness of the report format in helping children to develop logical scientific thinking. Here is one teacher's explanation:

> I try to point out the benefits of writing up experiments using the standard headings – I feel this is a logical way of presenting such work. I would not insist that they stick rigidly to the headings 'Aim, Method, etc.' but would look for a simple-to-follow logical presentation rather than a rambling essay.

This teacher went on to say that the various headings gave a focus to children's thought, and her views were echoed by most of the other members of the science department when we interviewed them.

To see how important the use of the format is in encouraging logical thinking, it is worth looking in some depth at examples of pupils' writing to examine the extent to which writing in the report format helps pupils to organize their thoughts. We looked at many examples from various science lessons. An analysis of the scripts showed that the 'Aim' of the experiment often proved straight-forward, as far as the children's accounts were concerned, mainly because it was often written down by the teacher beforehand, appearing as a title on the board, which the children copied directly into their books. The pupils' work therefore showed an *apparent* grasp of the purpose of their work, which was due to the fact that they rarely had to formulate the problem for themselves. 'Method' and 'Results' involved descriptive writing about what they had been told to do in class, or what they had observed the teacher doing. The greatest problem appeared with writing 'Conclusions', and some children omitted them altogether. Sometimes conclusions and results were mingled together and both appeared under the heading 'Results', but often conclusions as a summary of what had been achieved, or as the explanation of a principle, simply did not appear.

One lesson was concerned with the oxygen content of inhaled and exhaled air. The lesson had been lively, with the pupils enthusiastically involved with their experiments, and there had been discussion of each group's findings at the end of the lesson. The pupils then had to write reports of their experiments. An analysis of 20 marked scripts produced the following:

- 65 per cent of pupils reached a conclusion that was considered satisfactory by the teacher;
- 60 per cent of pupils wrote under a heading 'Conclusion'; and
- 50 per cent of pupils were able to express a conclusion, judged to be satisfactory, under the appropriate heading.

Figure 2.2 gives an extract from a pupil's description of the experiment. Having filled one gas jar with the normal classroom air, and a second gas jar with exhaled air, the pupils had to test for oxygen, using a lighted candle. Notice that the script has a correct conclusion, but the pupil has not conformed to the format, and does not give it recognition as a conclusion in the surface structure of his writing by using a separate heading and starting a new paragraph. However, it was obvious from reading this and other similar scripts from other lessons that the lack of a formal conclusion had in no way hampered some children's ability to draw inferences from the experiment. Cognitively, some pupils were capable of understanding scientific ideas, although they did not conform to the report format. Such examples stood in stark contrast to other scripts where conclusions were either omitted, or the pupils had wrongly concluded that there was more oxygen in exhaled air, a possible semantic confusion to which we shall return in the section on scientific terminology.

These results occurred when pupils had received oral instructions during the preceding lessons about how to write up reports and also had access to a booklet that gave them explicit instructions for writing up reports and specific guidance

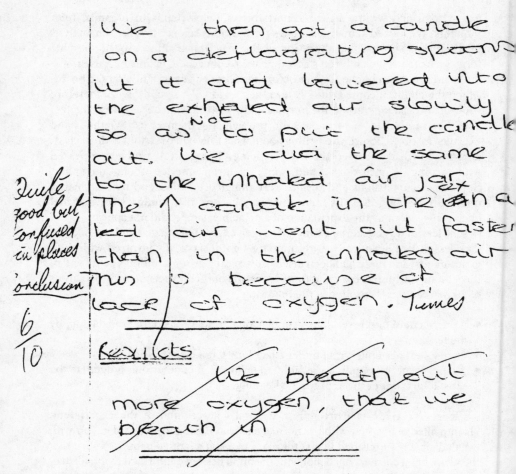

We then got a candle on a deflagrating spoon lit it and lowered into the exhaled air slowly so as not to put the candle out. We did the same to the inhaled air jar. The candle in the an an led air went out faster than in the unhaled air This is because of lack of oxygen. Times

Quite good but confused in places conclusion

6/10

Results

We breath out more oxygen, that we breath in

Figure 2.2 The oxygen content of inhaled and exhaled air
Confused report writing

on this particular experiment. Here are the instructions and the questions provided for pupils to refer to. They are written in a simple and 'chatty' style and appear to provide a clear-cut plan to follow:

To follow the experiment more easily, it is helpful to write up the experiment using subheadings:

AIM – tells you what the experiment is about or what you are trying to find out. It acts as a title.

DIAGRAM – shows simply and clearly how the apparatus was set up. This often saves a lot of time since you don't have to explain in words anything which is obvious from the diagram – just make a note in the METHOD section, 'see diagram'.

METHOD – is an account of how the experiment was performed. It should include all the details of what you did and any precautions taken, etc.

RESULTS – tell you what you saw happen or what you measured, etc.

CONCLUSION – is an explanation of WHY you got the results you did.

When you are writing up this experiment, first of all read through the following questions and try to include an explanation to each one in your writing up, unless your teacher tells you differently.

Questions
1 In the experiment, why were the gas jars used to collect the inhaled and exhaled air, the same size?
2 Why did you have to collect the exhaled air sample over water, instead of just breathing into a gas jar?
3 Why did you keep tops on the gas jars until you were ready to put the candles in?
4 Why did you put the candles on the deflagrating spoons into the gas jars slowly?
5 Is the lack of oxygen the only explanation of why the candles eventually went out? If you think not, suggest other reasons.
6 Why do you have to fill both gas jars with water before starting the experiment again?

Such a lesson seemed to augur well for written work, but the scripts showed that some pupils had considerable difficulty in either understanding or communicating the conclusion. There are three possible explanations for their problems. One may well be a lack of motivation and involvement with the task in hand, a point to which we return in our concluding chapter. Such an attitude might result in careless work on the part of some pupils. But most had completed the homework, handed it in and were looking forward in the next lesson to the teacher's marks and comments. In most cases, we therefore need to turn to two other possible explanations for their difficulties. Either they must have cognitive problems with the general concept of conclusions, or with the particular conclusion to this experiment. From the interviews and questionnaires it became apparent that the problem probably lay more in understanding the implications of particular experiments, rather than in an inability to understand the general concept. Many children were able to express themselves very clearly indeed on the general principle:

In the results we write down what happened and in the conclusion we write down why it happened.

. . . and *Conclusion* tells people what you have learnt.

. . . and a short paragraph about what you learnt or found out these are commonly called the conclusion.

Even those replies that were ambiguous in the questionnaires were clarified during interviews.

The evidence from this set of scripts does not therefore necessarily support the teachers' views that writing in the approved format assists pupils' understanding. Pupils had certainly learnt what conclusions were supposed to be, but found significant difficulty in relating this generalized knowledge to their work in the particular lesson. Secondly, some of those who did work out the conclusion could not order their thinking to conform with the demands of the format. In the sample of scripts their problems with the format made their learning appear to be less than it in fact was, in terms of the content of the lesson. What is interesting is that all this happened when the pupils had been given a great deal of instruction about the conclusion to their work and the format of their report, both in class discussion and in guiding questions in their booklet. By all the usual indicators this was a well-organized and successful lesson, and yet the written accounts did not conform with the teacher's expectations in many cases.

We might therefore conclude a number of things from this investigation. First, in any lesson, a number of pupils do not understand the conclusion of their experiments because they do not understand the question they are asking (the aim), or how the method and results relate to it. Secondly, if teachers continue to demand the report format, then we must think of more effective ways of teaching pupils how to write within this convention. Thirdly, if they understand anyway, perhaps the science report format is not such a vitally important learning aid and it need not be employed every time children put pen to paper in science. Of course, it would be foolhardy to conclude from a few small samples of work that the traditional format is unsatisfactory as a teaching aid. In fact it would be impossible to prove the case by experimentation, as that would require a series of samples over a long period of time, coupled with extensive interviews, and even so any improvement in logical thinking would not necessarily be attributable to making children write in the report format. What we can say is that, while using the report format may be helpful to some children, it may not be to others; indeed, it may serve only to constrict their thinking. In addition, some children can think logically without it, as they displayed their understanding in their written work, even though not within the format. We know, for example, from the research of Bereiter and Scardamalia (1982) that teaching children to write logically involves much more than simply giving them concepts like 'conclusion', and samples like this seem to support this view.

Therefore, should we be looking for rigid format writing and penalize children who don't use it? Or should we be more sensitive to the many factors that may affect children's ability to learn in science? In the face of the extent of pupils' difficulties that we can observe in this and many other science lessons, it may well be worth considering other types of written work that may help children to learn, rather than restricting their opportunities by offering only one type of writing that only a limited number of pupils may find useful.

Impersonal language

Next, we should like to consider one of the main characteristics of the kind of language we found being used by children in their writing in science. This is the use of impersonal prose, including a preference among some teachers for the passive voice, 'The test-tube was placed . . .' being preferred to 'We placed the test-tube . . .', for example. Most teachers interviewed expressed a preference for impersonal writing and disliked the idea of what they considered to be irrelevant and personal remarks entering into children's writing. They believed that, like using the 'report' format, the use of impersonal language would also encourage children to think in a scientific way. Most of the teachers expressed their preference for the passive voice (which they sometimes misleadingly referred to as the 'past tense' – a phrase that some of the children also learnt to use to describe this kind of style). Here is one example of a teacher who had very precise expectations: 'I expect a written report in the past tense – a detached observation of all that occurred.' This teacher quoted an example that had recently horrified her:

> We put the card on a pin. Then we put the pin in a cork. Then we fastened the cork into the clamp like Mrs. _____ did.!!! [teacher's exclamation marks]

Similar disapproval by another teacher showed in the marking of one pupil's work: 'Then a thermometer was given to us and we were told not to break it "<u>or else</u>".' The teacher has underlined 'or else'.

Only two teachers in the department deviated slightly from this general consensus. One said, 'For instance, if they write something and then write "Yuk! I didn't like it", I'll accept that.' However, in the scripts from this teacher's class that we studied, such personal comments never appeared, and in lessons he emphasized the importance of impersonal language. The second teacher, who was also the one who had shown least concern about the need for his pupils to use the 'report' format, favoured the use of impersonal language but tolerated 'lapses'. However, he expressed the hope that children would gradually develop an impersonal style during the course of the year. The main difference between his approach and that of the others was his confidence in the children's ability to develop this writing technique for themselves.

Many of the pupils had a clear understanding of the kind of language preferred by their teachers, and the responses from different classes when they were asked about this tended to vary, depending on the particular teachers they had been taught by, who had slightly different demands and communicated these to the pupils. By the time the pupils were interviewed, they were well into their work in the third year of secondary schooling and had absorbed a generalized picture of the kind of writing that was expected in science. This picture was a product both of their experiences in their middle schools and in their work so far in their upper school. They could explain the demands clearly (though there was, of course, some repetition of their teachers' mistaken description of the passive transformation as the 'past tense'), but they were not necessarily aware of why they were writing in this way:

> If you put 20 cc of water into a test-tube, you don't put – um – 'We put 20 cc of water into a test-tube'. '20 cc of water were put in a test-tube'. You do it in the past tense. I don't know why though.
>
> And you never do it as though you're doing it. It's just always sort of 'It was done'.

Other pupils thought that the reason for using impersonal language was connected with needing the basic facts for revision purposes, a reason that matched exactly with the concerns of some of the teachers:

> You've got to just put down the basic facts. If you keep going on about how it happened and sort of describe this, they tell you there's too much description. You've just got to keep to the facts. Just to give the basic things. Because you come back to revise and if you've got all descriptive writing like you do in English and things and it's going to be worse for revising because the fancy words are coming in that aren't the facts.

This is a good example of a pupil who considers that the writing in science makes up a kind of revision notebook, which will be most effective if it is brief and to the point. It is useful to be aware of the importance of this purpose of their writing for many of the pupils and their teachers because of their awareness of the need for both internal and external examination success.

There was considerable embarrassment on the part of some pupils about past occasions when they had not been so sensitive to the teachers' demands:

> When writing science and I did 'then the metal balance could fit snugly back in its home', and all this that I wrote about. Do you remember that? [laughter] ... In Physics or something. . . . It was just like a story – you know: 'How the metal bar cooled down'. . . . Yeh. And that's what I'd sort of done. I felt a right nana [laughter].

The pupils were also aware of the need to choose their adjectives carefully:

> P1: [You can be?] descriptive in English, can't you sort of, but in science I don't.
> P2: It's a lovely pink colour. [laughter]
> P3: They wouldn't take to that.
> P1: You don't call it that kind of colour, though. Cos if it's violet you write it down that it's pink or red. You know, a basic colour like. There was one that we wrote down that was aubergine ... and. . . . He nearly died. 'You mean it's gone pink, don't you?'. You know you can't sort of.
> I: Why do you think that is? Why don't they like you to write aubergine?
> P1: Because they've been taught not to and therefore they don't want cos I suppose when they went to school, I know it sound awful but they didn't do as much as we do now like description and things like that.

P2: I mean you don't get marks for being descriptive in science but you do in English. I mean it depends what lesson you're in. I think it is really.

So now we have two more reasons given by the pupils for using impersonal language: one is the factor of 'tradition' that we discussed early on in the chapter, and the other is a more instrumental one – in science lessons you only get marks for science.

Not all of the pupils could articulate the teachers' expectations in the clear and explicit way that the pupils above were capable of, but this did not mean that they were unaware of them in their writing. Some pupils, whose scripts showed that they were observing the appropriate rules, did not mention them voluntarily, and some had difficulty in explaining even when prompted. Many pupils remarked that they found it difficult to talk about these things because they did not usually think about them. And there were, of course, many pupils who did not master all the subtleties of writing their accounts in impersonal prose.

The teachers had clear justifications for their advocacy of impersonal language. It was valued as an aid to the children's thought processes, and as an important part of learning in science. They felt that mixing scientific thought and personal feelings would confuse the children. The use of impersonal language was seen as a way of allowing and encouraging children to focus their minds on the scientific question in hand. Impersonal language was, therefore, equated with adopting a 'scientific perspective'. Here is an extract from an interview with one teacher where the importance of impersonal language is being stressed:

> . . . I get the feeling that writing in the third person possibly leads to a greater clarity of thought and expression. Um. I'm trying hopefully to end up with a piece of written work that's written objectively rather than subjectively. Um. I'm not really after an expressive style as possibly we might be wanting in English. We're not wanting a creative style. We're wanting – er – very definitive statements, short, crisp, to the point, without any padding. I get the feeling that that comes out better written in that way.

The teachers in no way wanted to deprive the children of their subjective experiences, and make them unfeelingly objective. But they felt that the expression of feelings or any subjective comments in their writing might interfere with the development of scientific attitudes and cognitive styles. Consequently, interdisciplinary learning and integrated approaches had a particular meaning for some of these teachers that was rather different from the progressive concepts of integrated, interdisciplinary learning. This was clearly shown in the view of one of the teachers, who saw English lessons as the appropriate place for the expression of feelings associated with work done in science, as an extract from our field notes shows:

> I mentioned to the teacher the Schools Council view that personal reactions to work done in science could be a part of children's writing. She said she would like to see

more cooperation between the Science and English departments so that when, for example, children had dissected a rat in Biology, they could write it up from the scientific point of view and then in their English lessons write about their personal reactions to it. Children might not gain an understanding of the scientific perspective if they spent too much time describing their thoughts and feelings.

And this extract also highlights another major concern: too much time spent on 'creative' writing in science will mean that too little time is devoted to the acquisition of scientific knowledge. It echoes a widespread concern among teachers about the limited time available to teach the content and skills required in specialist subjects, and the consequent restrictions that this places on the choice of teaching method.

However, the concerns voiced by the teacher mentioned above, and many other teachers, include their very definite view that cognitive development in science is hampered by the inclusion of what they considered to be the non-scientific aspects of classroom experience, in children's writing. Impersonal language and the use of the passive voice had far more importance than just creating an impression of objectivity. So, what we need to consider now is what exactly teachers mean by a 'scientific perspective' and look in a little more detail at the place of impersonal writing in its development.

In talking to children about how to write up their reports teachers tended to use remarks like 'Only include the IMPORTANT points.' This served as a shorthand for 'Only include the scientific aspects – I'm not interested in your feelings or personal experiences.' Distinguishing the teacher's conception of what was important in the lesson was, therefore, a difficult but essential skill that each child needed to acquire in order to be successful at doing science. It involves far more than being impersonal in the sense of eliminating emotional reactions, or remarks about whom the child worked with in a particular lesson. For example, in the remark about the thermometer quoted earlier, breaking it is obviously important to both parties in the practicalities of classroom life, but is not important within the framework of the 'scientific' report. Thus, of course, what is involved is the adoption by the pupils of the teacher's way of looking at the lesson and its purposes. The teacher's perspective comprises a number of cognitive frameworks of rules about thinking scientifically, plus ideas about teaching objectives for a particular lesson. It is these collections of rules that pupils need to gain access to if they are to master the cognitive demands of the lesson. In addition, of course, they have to conform to the rules about written work and how it should be presented.

The point about cognitive frameworks is most clearly illustrated by a rather extreme case of a pupil failing to adopt the same kind of understanding of the lesson as his teacher. The example below is the complete report of a science experiment written by a 'low-ability' pupil who obviously had little concept of the teacher's frameworks:

Today in Biology we did an experiment on inhaled and exhaled air and this is what we did. We got two glass tubes and we put some water in it and we got a candle and we lit it and put it in a glass tube like this:

[DIAGRAM OF GAS JAR DRAWN HERE]

That is a diagram to show what we did this morning. Then we got a big tray and filled it with water and I enjoyed watching it this morning and it was a good experiment and I like Biology.

Here the pupil is using expressive rather than impersonal language, but this is not the reason for his failure to adopt a scientific perspective. The use of impersonal language will not rescue pupils from misinterpretations such as these. What has happened is that he has failed utterly to understand the question that the teacher was asking – the scientific principle that the practical work was intended to illustrate – and thus he was unable to operate within her interpretive framework. For him it was a busy and interesting lesson, but he has no idea of the point at issue. So here we have an important example of one aspect of what it means to operate, or fail to operate, from a scientific perspective. In this case, it means complete failure to understand the aim of the experiment.

But difficulties in adopting a scientific approach are not always so wholesale. A detailed study of other examples shows the importance of remembering that the concept of a 'scientific perspective', because it is such an all-embracing term and such a handy phrase to use, actually masks the heterogeneous collection of rules that are operating, and to which children must conform.

Consider, for instance, what is happening in the two contrasting pieces of writing below. In this particular chemistry lesson, which was their first at their new school, the pupils had been learning how a bunsen burner works. They were asked to write about the three different types of flame produced by the bunsen burner. Because it was their first lesson, the teacher did not necessarily expect them to use impersonal language or the scientific report style. They were asked to work as follows:

Right now, here's your homework. All this is to be done in the front of your notebooks.

Number one – heading – The Bunsen Burner.

Number two – neat half page diagram, in pencil, of the bunsen burner.

Next point – describe the three flame types and what you think you use each for.

And the last point – How could you prove which area of the bunsen flame is the hottest?

All this is to be done in full sentences – best English. We don't use half sentences.

We have chosen the reports from a 'more able' girl and a 'less able' boy, using the terms loosely in the usual staffroom evaluation of these pupils. The more able girl began with a brisk and scientific sounding start. She then moved into a thorough description of each type of flame, using more personal language, but maintaining a scientific approach to her observations:

Description
There are three types of flame, the luminous flame, the half luminous and the non-luminous. The luminous being the coolest and the non-luminous being the hottest.

The luminous flame – The colour is a goldy orange-yellow colour. It is about as big as an average ruler (about 30 cms). It hasn't really got a shape but if you were to describe it, it is a sort of long bending shape. It makes a soft hissing sound. The air hole is shut.

The half luminous flame – The colour is a light transparent blue. The size is 25 cm long and much more straight. There is also more of a hissing sound. The air-hole is half open.

The non-luminous flame – The colour is a transparent blue you can hardly see. The size is about the same as the luminous flame. The flame is long, straight and very thin. The hissing is quite strong.

You could use the luminous flame for just warming things up. The half luminous flame could be used for some test tube experiments. The non-luminous flame could be used for experiments that need a lot of warming up and heat.

The main difference between the luminous and the non-luminous flame is that the luminous is the same temperature all over. But the non-luminous is different temperatures all over, the hottest being 850°C.

You could prove which is the hottest by getting a pair of test tube holders and by getting hold of a piece of special paper with the holders and taking it up and down the flame and seeing when the paper singes or burns the most.

Apart from one or two inaccuracies, this is a well-rounded account, and certainly no mean feat for a first lesson, when there is so much to take in. Her main fault is to neglect to mention the use of the luminous flame as a safety flame. During the lesson it was strongly emphasized by the teacher that the luminous flame was to be used whenever the bunsen burner was alight but not being used to heat things, as it was then clearly visible to everyone that the burner was on.

Now let us see how our second pupil responded to this lesson:

This week's Chemistry lesson I thought the best I had, because I never had Chemistry before.

Luminous Non-Luminous. If a non-luminous bunsen burner was on everyone who went past would be able to see it. If a luminous bunsen burner was on everybody, a boy or a girl would think it was of[f] and they would touch it and burn they hand. Or if a girl next to the bunsen burner leans over it, she would think it was off and she would of burned her hair.

To prove this we would get a test tube and turn the bunsen burner of[f] and put it into the middle of the gas test and thoroughly turn on the tap and light a match and the gas would travel through the tube.

Apart from his delightfully ambiguous start, his mind has focused almost entirely on the importance of safety in the laboratory. The rest of his writing discusses the bunsen flames in this context (and because of his ignorance of whether the word luminous means 'giving out light' or 'invisible', he also appears to lack understanding when in fact he does not). Even though he and the girl had both copied down the teacher's instructions, which provided a framework for the writing, he has only glanced at anything other than the safety aspect. He was a well-motivated pupil, who had spent considerable time on this work and produced a beautifully detailed diagram, so it was not a lack of effort that produced this one-sided account.

These two pieces of writing raise a number of interesting points. First, in this task, and presumably many others, the use of impersonal language does not seem to be particularly relevant to the development of the pupils' powers of observation. What seems to be far more important is their particular perception of the lesson. They see different things, and emphasize different points. They are choosing to take certain things out of it. This idea is something we shall return to in the discussion of imaginative writing later in this chapter. What it is important to realize is how individual each pupil's response is to what goes on in the lesson, and the importance of those different perceptions of certain elements of the lesson in creating the appearance of success or failure in developing a scientific perspective.

For example, the point we mentioned earlier about cognitive frameworks and teaching objectives is also neatly illustrated by another chemistry lesson. The topic for the lesson was the boiling point of water, and groups of pupils did their own observations on this, measuring the boiling point of water and then seeing if it was affected by the addition of some salt. One pupil's conclusion was judged by the teacher to be 'confused' because she had not reformulated the aim of her experiment in order to write a conclusion that specifically stated that impurities in the form of salt made the water boil at a higher temperature. Instead, she had represented the complex reality thus:

> We didn't come to a definite conclusion because we all had different answers, because some of the water may not have had bits in and others may have, or the pyrex beaker may have been dirty. We all got different conclusions for salt water too because sir could have put more salt in some of them.

The teacher explained that the pupil here had received lower marks because she had not 'centred' on the particular purpose of the experiment. Another pupil who had written '*Conclusion:* when we added the salt to the water the temperature rose', received a higher mark and the comment 'Good Effort'. The teacher here has accepted this mere description as an adequate conclusion by reading into it what the pupil had actually left implicit – the principle that salt affects the boiling point of water. The pupil who was 'confused' had been thinking very scientifically about the factors that might affect the validity of the experiment, but the teacher had overlooked that because of his concern that she should conform exactly to his planned objectives for this particular lesson – to understand the *increase* in boiling point that salt produces. Here we have more clues about what is really meant by teachers when they voice their concern about pupils not thinking scientifically unless they use impersonal language – teachers have precise lesson objectives, and want the pupils to reproduce these in the required written form.

We know that one of the science teachers' worries is that retelling personal incidents about the lesson may displace some important scientific ideas that are the real focus of the lesson. But in addition there is the idea that pupils won't 'think straight' about the scientific principles or processes involved if their descriptions are contaminated with emotive words or phrases relating to what they were doing. By trying to filter out everything except those processes and principles, pupils' minds should be able to comprehend them more easily. They are thus arguing that pupils can cue in to the collections of ground rules that comprise the scientific enterprise more easily if they ignore what is going on in the rest of the world.

To assess the validity of that kind of argument, we have to look at how we come to understand different sets of ground rules. How do we move into different frames? For the moment it seems a reasonable assumption that it helps the acquisition of a new set of ground rules if you put to one side the other sets you have been using, and which have provided you with other perceptions of the situation. In addition, scientific understanding includes the logic associated with those rules – it may be the moment when something 'clicks', when ideas and experiences rearrange themselves into an order that makes sense according to those collections of rules that we call scientific thinking. From examining the sort of errors pupils make it appears that 'scientific thinking' or the 'scientific perspective' as a whole is not usually the problem. It seems more sensible if we believe that the concept of a 'subject perspective' is in reality a shorthand way of referring to complex systems of rules about tasks, i.e. the systems we have chosen in this book refer to as 'frameworks'. When we examine situations where things go wrong for children we often find that the problem lies in understanding one or more of the assumptions that they need to make in order to complete their tasks. And sometimes, some of the rules they have to operate by may be difficult to grasp because they are unfamiliar or because they contradict common sense. These sorts of failures then produce the phenomenon of an 'unscientific' attitude.

An excellent example of one kind of inability to switch frames can be found in a biology lesson that was part of our study. The topic for the lesson was the 'Characteristic of a Living Thing'. First, the various characteristics of a living organism had been discussed, such as growth, feeding, respiration, etc. For their homework, the pupils were asked to devise a set of scientific tests to prove whether or not a bunch of keys might be living. This caused considerable merriment among some of the class, and we guessed that it would produce some interesting scripts, which it indeed did.

Some of the pupils were interviewed after we had had a chance to look at their homework, and it had also been marked. During the course of the interviews we talked about the reaction of some people in the class and began to ask the pupils if they thought the task had been a sensible one or not. This was something of a leading question, but was used deliberately to make it clear to the pupils that it would be all right to criticize the task if they wanted to. The pupils' responses varied greatly, and illustrate clearly what particular rules they were keeping to in their interpretation of it.

A number of pupils found difficulty, or seemed inhibited about, devising tests for the bunch of keys because they were bound to an everyday commonsense interpretation of the task. They could not operate according to the mode of scientific enquiry because the answer seemed so obvious, and some of them thought the teacher was 'daft' even to bother with such an idea:

> We already know they aren't living. . . . It's a fact of life they aren't living. That's all we know about them. . . . I don't really see why you should test them when you already know the answer.

Another pupil had found the task so incomprehensible that he had asked his Dad, and father and son had together concocted the following piece of writing:

> A bunch of keys are inanimate objects and are manufactured by man from mineral ore which does not have the ability of growth, movement, reproduction or sensitivity. Mineral ores do not breathe, feed or excrete.

Some pupils could not see the sense of testing the bunch of keys to see if it was alive, but accepted the idea of testing something living, e.g. a mouse. Their thinking seemed to depend on the commonsense idea that the mouse *could* be living *or* dead, while in the everyday world there is obviously no chance that the bunch of keys is going to be alive.

In contrast, another pupil showed an excellent understanding of the task, even to the extent of using his teacher as a 'control'. But he also saw the task as so unusual that it was a good opportunity to have something of a joke at the teacher's expense:

> to see whether the keys are alive in contrast with mr X
>
> Breathe   We could simply watch the chest and stomach of Mr X if he was breathing his chest would move in and out. then do the same with the keys.
>
> Move   Again, wat[c]h both subjects.
>
> Sensitivity   To[u]ch each subject with a piece of red hot iron and *listen* to the result.
>
> Grow   We could take down recordings of each subjects measurements each year and read the results.
>
> Reproduce   We could place a female in front of mr X (attractive) and another bunch of keys in front of the others and watch.

Feed   We could deprive each subject of food for three weeks then seat them
              down to a fiest and watch.

Excrete   After doing the previous test then deprive them both of opportunities
              of going to the wc for a couple of days.

But although he had been able to complete the task to the teacher's satisfaction,
when interviewed he too rejected it as a stupid thing to do:

> Bit stupid, innit. . . . Well, you can tell a bunch of keys isn't alive, can't you? You can
> pick it up and shake it about. . . . He said if some aliens land on this planet. That's a
> bit stupid as well, cos I don' think they ever could do.

Finally, another pupil had treated the task as sensible and serious, and done his
best to devise tests appropriate for the bunch of keys. The previous pupil had
rejected the teacher's ideas about aliens from another planet wanting to find out
about life on earth, and needing to test the bunch of keys. However, this
justification of the task had captured the other pupil's imagination and provided
him with a way in to understanding the principles underlying scientific
investigation:

> *I:*   Did you think it was a sensible idea to think about a bunch of keys and a human
>   being and – er – whether one was alive or not?
> *P:*   Er, the way he put it about being somebody from another planet exploring this
>   place, yes it would. Quite all right, yeah . . . 'cos er, well, if they wanted to find
>   out about us they might try to communicate with a bunch of keys first and they
>   wouldn't get as much response and that.
> *I:*   That's an interesting idea, isn't it. Mmm. Is there any other reason why it's a
>   sensible idea to do that apart from thinking about people coming from outer
>   space?
> *P:*   Well, yes, er, if we're going to find out anything about what's happening around
>   us, we want to find out whether things are living.

Such a pupil demonstrates the ability to engage in imaginative hypothetical
thinking of the 'what if?' kind we referred to in Chapter 1. He is able to suspend
commonsense interpretive frameworks in favour of those preferred by scientific
method. For, in this instance, that is the nature of 'scientific thinking'.

The examples we have used during the course of this discussion on the use of
impersonal language seem to indicate that the ability to think scientifically does
not depend on using impersonal language to describe the learning that is taking
place, but is centrally dependent on the ability to accept particular rules about
how to think about various aspects of an issue, especially when those rules seem
to go against commonsense, everyday interpretations. It is possible, of course,
that some pupils may be helped to do this if they use prose that makes them cast
aside many of the everyday experiences and rules that are part of their store of
knowledge. But now that we have analysed more clearly what the 'scientific
perspective' actually seems to consist of, we are also free to suggest that there

seems to be no reason why a wide variety of personal and impersonal language should not be used in the course of doing science in school. Of course, teachers are quite right to say that 'creative' writing that emphasizes only subjective feelings and responses must not be allowed to dominate, and prevent the development of scientific thinking and writing. But that is quite a different thing from arguing that scientific thinking will only develop through the exclusive use of impersonal language. It seems that there is plenty of room for the colour 'aubergine', and no good reason why children should not tell us simply and directly what they did, rather than hobbling about in the stilted language of the passive transformation, whose difficulties might disturb their train of thought even more than a passing reference to some amusing classroom incident. And if they mention the people they were working with, or a dropped thermometer, might this not in the long term produce a more useful revision aid, because on re-reading their accounts, they may have a more vivid recollection of some of the scientific aspects of their work as well? These comments are not meant to be an argument for the entire abolition of impersonal prose. There is no reason why it cannot take its place among the range of writing techniques pupils are capable of using. And certainly, it is an important skill to be able, when the occasion demands it, to present a written account that is a concise impersonal summary of work done, and the level of scientific understanding achieved. But, in certain situations, and with certain learners, it may be more appropriate to encourage other ways of writing. This is therefore an argument for flexibility and variety, and for teachers to be confident in the knowledge that children's ability to reason scientifically will not necessarily be hampered.

We hope that this discussion has begun to clarify the nature of some of the learning processes in science and the relationship between thought and language in this area, as far as impersonal language is concerned, but of course there are other aspects of scientific language still to consider, and it is to these we now turn.

Scientific terminology

Even more than using impersonal language, most subject teachers place great importance on the use of specialist terms and the normal vocabulary of their subject. This is particularly true of most science teachers. Preferred words seem to range along a continuum. At one end are specialist terms that many teachers consider essential for the pupils' understanding. (This is an interesting idea that we shall explore in more detail after our discussion of some pupils' work.) At the other end of the continuum are those words that are preferred terms simply because they sound more scientific than their everyday counterparts.

The teachers in our study varied in their attitude to the question of scientific terminology. One of the science teachers did not like to burden children with what he considered to be unnecessary jargon. He said that, together with a former colleague, he had worked out a minimum number of technical terms that pupils needed to know for examination purposes, and that these were systematically taught. Apart from that, he tried not to make too many demands on the children as far as scientific vocabulary was concerned. His reasoning was as follows:

> Well, very often they'll, if they're worrying about the technical language, they don't describe what they saw because they're so, you know, worried about what the flask is called, and it stops them actually getting on with what was the important thing, which was what went on inside the beaker, if you know what I mean. . . . So they get caught up with the . . . fringe details and miss the important point of the experiment. Now if at the end of one important experiment, they get one idea out of it, I think I'd be not too worried if they'd called a beaker a jar.

However, other teachers placed much heavier demands on their pupils and encouraged pupils to use the conventions of scientific vocabulary. Here is an extract from a biology lesson where the teacher is conveying messages about some of the subtleties of the scientific style:

> *T:*   [writing on board] . . . To make – I prefer the word 'prepare' but nevertheless I'll accept the word 'make' – an animal slide and examine it . . .

In order to write successfully for most teachers, children learn to be sensitive to the teacher's deliberate presentation of new terms, even when the teacher does not make reference to the fact that the children's writing ought to include them. Clues about the type of vocabulary to use are being given all the time:

> *T:*   What's happening?
> *P1:* It's effervescing.
> *T:*   [Expressing mock surprise] . . . Yeh! [Then acting dumb] What does that mean?
> *P2:* It's all frothing up.
> *T:*   Yes [jokingly] it's all froffing up.

In this extract, the teacher shows that she values the technical term, first by expressing surprise that anyone should know such a 'posh' word as 'effervescing' and then by mocking its commonplace counterpart – 'froffing' – she signals her approval of its use. Her attitude, and the fact that she demanded an explanation of the term for the benefit of those who did not know it, are cues that the pupils needed to pick up, so that they could incorporate the word in their writing.

Pupils can be very adept at picking up and using new terminology. A chemistry lesson showed the process in action particularly clearly. The lesson was concerned with immiscible liquids such as oil and water, and how they might be separated. The teacher wrote a heading 'Separating Immiscible Liquids' on the board, but did not directly explain the meaning of the term at any subsequent point during the lesson, which involved a problem-solving exercise on the topic. In the classwork writing that followed, some pupils simply referred to 'the liquid' or 'the two liquids' that had been the subject of their investigation. Others, however, began to work out for themselves that there must be a link between what they were doing and the mysterious word on the board and, without reference to the teacher, began to incorporate the word in their writing.

We do know that sometimes the introduction of a technical word, especially a long one (and aren't they all!), can confuse a child and create the appearance that they misunderstand when in fact they do not. This was obviously the case in the example we quoted in the discussion on impersonal language, when the pupil involved transposed 'luminous' and 'non-luminous' because they were terms he had not come across before. Similarly, some pupils looking at the carbon dioxide content of 'inhaled' and 'exhaled' air had problems coming to grips with these two new words. In the following case, however, we do not know for sure if this pupil really got it wrong or just got his terminology muddled up. The rest of his report is a description of what he did, and there is no other way in which the writing by itself can provide any clues about whether he understood or not.

Conclusion: We got this result because inhaled air had less carbon dioxide in it.

[*Teacher's comment:* A large cross through the work.]

It is interesting to note the unhelpfulness of the teacher's response here, which may have been a result of lack of time for marking, or a misunderstanding of the pupil's needs.

Even bearing in mind these difficulties, there is a justification for increasing pupils' vocabulary so far as words which can be used to facilitate scientific description and explanation are concerned, while minimizing the need for superfluous 'jargonese'. But we need to consider carefully why this needs to be done. Some writers, like many of the teachers, believe that there is an inextricable link between the words used and the ideas people are capable of thinking about. Advocates of such a view (e.g. Richards, 1978) argue that scientific concepts can only be properly understood through learning the associated specialist terminology. This is not a view that we share, because a concept can be grasped and described in writing before it is 'christened' with a specialist word or phrase. Some of the previous examples illustrate this point quite clearly, and even show how pupil's explanations may be confused precisely because they have had to grapple with unfamiliar terminology. None the less there is a virtue in the use of certain specialist terms in the sense that, correctly employed to identify a specialist concept, they can often be a more 'economical' use of language, as Edwards (1974) has pointed out. But the introduction of new words needs to be done sparingly if it is to enhance understanding, rather than confuse pupils.

Selective explicitness

Descriptions of experiments and explanations of scientific concepts and principles are, of course, usually produced by pupils so that teachers can assess them, first to judge the level of their pupils' knowledge and understanding and, secondly, to formally record and grade their ability and progress. In all subjects it is important that pupils understand this process and adopt writing styles that maximize their chances of receiving a favourable judgement from the teacher. The teachers we studied used the marks, grades and examination results in the third year for reports and also to make recommendations about the most appropriate course for the pupils in the fourth and fifth years, which led to external examinations. Because most of the teachers only saw the third-year classes once a week, and each class had an average of 30 pupils, there was little opportunity to get to know the pupils individually. Therefore, the teachers relied heavily on information they had recorded in their mark books, and this was exclusively a record of written performance in class and homework exercises, or in tests. Even though this situation may well change to a certain extent in the future with the advent of records of achievement, which place more emphasis on oral skills and practical abilities, it is still fair to say that written work is likely to retain its primacy in most schemes of assessment.

Bernstein (1971b) emphasized long ago the importance of an elaborated code of speech for success in schools, but the importance of an elaborated code in writing rather than in oral communication was not an issue that he addressed. Bernstein's work can be useful, however, in drawing our attention to the fact that certain children seem to be more successful than others in using a ground rule that is important for school success. The rule is one about the need to provide an 'elaborate' or 'explicit' account for teachers, whether in oral or written work. As we indicated in our introduction, we consider that Bernstein's hypothesis of two distinct language codes needs to be questioned and that the concept of ground rules is a more effective analytical tool; therefore, perhaps elaborated code is not really the appropriate phrase for the skill we are about to discuss. Rather, it is the ability to produce writing that is a display of knowledge, and that exhibits elaboration and explicitness in certain precisely defined ways.

Some pupils were much more adept at delivering the required type of 'selective explicitness' than others. In explanatory accounts there is always the danger of infinite regression, as you attempt to decide what to include and what you can assume the reader knows. But pupils also had to remember their obligation to 'show off' their knowledge to the right degree. They had to work out a fine balance between:

1 What they can take for granted the teacher knows.
2 What they can take for granted the teacher knows that the pupil already knows.
3 What needs to be stated explicitly to the teacher, to prove that the pupil knows it.

Thus the pupils in the lesson on the oxygen content of air had to include an explanation of why they had used gas jars of the same size, although there was no need to explain what a gas jar was. When one pupil wrote 'We took two gas jars of the same size', the teacher responded 'Why?' in the margin. A second pupil explained in her account '. . . because we could have got a different answer', and again this was queried because it had not sufficiently displayed the girl's level of understanding. A more successful attempt by another pupil was rewarded with a tick: 'They must be the same size so there is an equal amount of air in each.'

In each case here the teacher had given clues about what was wrong or right with the writing. However, with one lesson a week and 30 pupils to attend to in each class, and a syllabus to get through, there was little time for most teachers to systematically help pupils to develop this skill. On top of that, most teachers did not recognize the need to spend much time on developing these aspects of pupils' competence in writing. Mostly, the reports the pupils had written were not discussed in the following lessons, so the extent to which pupils absorbed the requirements for this task were dependent on the teachers' sporadic attention to it, their often cryptic marking, and the extent to which pupils thought it important to attend to those messages.

Interviews with some pupils began to reveal this problem of insensitivity to the demands of the teacher audience. Two pupils, who were interviewed about the accounts they had written on the different types of bunsen burner flame, had adopted an inappropriate framework for the task. Like one of the examples previously discussed, these pupils had neglected to mention in their writing that the yellow luminous flame was a 'safety flame', although in the interview they explained clearly when and why it was used. When asked why they had not included these points in their reports, their replies suggested that they had made a judgement using a 'commonsense' framework of rules rather than considering the 'classroom' framework and what the teacher would want to know they had learned:

I: Why do you think you left that out?
P: Because, um, it was used – if you use your common sense, well, um, you would put it on the yellow flame instead of the blue flame.

Of course, some pupils tend to go to the opposite extreme and become over-elaborate. One pupil in this sample was reprimanded by the teacher for writing too much.

In the light of these remarks it is instructive to look at the comments of other researchers who have used examples of children's writing. Sometimes they have behaved rather like teachers, and relied too much on the writing when trying to assess the children's cognitive development. Let us look at some writing discussed by Jill Richards (1978), bearing in mind the points we have raised above. Richards is a strong advocate of the use of impersonal language and scientific terminology in science lessons, and she is concerned that children's conceptual development will be hampered unless specialist language is used.

Here Richards (1978, p. 112) discusses some examples where pupils were told to write down how and what an earth worm eats:

> The question on feeding consistently provided responses that demonstrated differences in individual conceptual development associated with ability rather than chronological age. The following examples, which are typical, are drawn from the 14+ age group.
>
> BELOW-AVERAGE ABILITY:
>   'It eats soil as it goes through the soil.'
> AVERAGE ABILITY:
>   'As it burrows through the soil decayed plant matter is taken in at the front end and passes through the body. Waste is removed at the anus.'
> ABOVE-AVERAGE ABILITY:
>   'The earthworm takes in dead vegetation in the soil that enters its mouth as it burrows in the ground. The soil passes down a long tube and the goodness is taken from it leaving the waste which passes out of the anus as worm casts.'

Bearing in mind the points we have made above about competent communicators being those pupils who know how to be selectively explicit, we might be able to explain Richards's examples by saying that the average and below-average pupils did not know that they had to give very detailed answers. What they have written is not wrong; it is just rather brief. We do not know from the evidence presented whether they were able to write longer answers or not. Maybe, as in our own examples above, they thought certain things were obvious, or just common sense and did not need mentioning. What they certainly lack is sensitivity to the requirements of their audience. Most teachers are aware that it is characteristic of less able pupils to write little compared with more able pupils. What they often seem to lack is a mental framework or structure of questions to ask themselves about what ought to be included in their accounts. For years CSE examiners took account of this in all subjects by devising tightly structured questions to ask candidates, rather than relying on the short open-ended questions more characteristic of GCE. (For a further discussion of this point, see the section on 'Essays and accounts' in Chapter 3.) We can conclude here, then, that there is little definite evidence for a lack of conceptual development, but plenty of evidence for a lack of written communication skills, in the sense that they have not identified or used the appropriate ground rules.

Richards also asserts that the examples show the need for scientific and technical language in concept development. If we look at the writing, however, we can't see much evidence of the lack of technical language being responsible for the children's difficulties. Consider the explanation 'It eats soil'. Worms most certainly do ingest soil. The above-average pupil uses the words 'takes in' to refer to the fact that the worm digests mainly the vegetable matter in the soil. Nothing brilliantly technical about that phrase. It is a more *detailed* account, but the language is still an everyday vocabulary. The more able pupil continues 'and the goodness is taken from it'. Again, a more detailed description of the sequence of processes; but surely these words would also be known to the less able pupils? Once more, what the more able pupil is certainly very good at is displaying his/her knowledge.

Of course, this is not to deny that any increase in vocabulary, whether scientific or general, is bound to enhance anyone's ability to explain concepts. But that doesn't appear to be the root cause of the differences in the writing in these examples. What they tell us is that we must be very careful not to take it for granted that what pupils write down is all that they know.

The more we begin to appreciate these points, the more examples we can find, practically everywhere we turn, whether it is during the normal routine of classroom teaching, or in the examples used in published texts. For example, Wade and Wood (1979) touch on the problem of these hidden rules of communicative competence, but without fully articulating it in their conclusions. They compare the way two pupils have completed science worksheets (see Fig. 2.3). One pupil, at first glance, appears to be much better at science than the other, because his prose is more explicit, and he shows more audience awareness by explaining his thinking clearly for the teacher. Wade and Wood warn that this facility with language can often be mistaken for a better level of scientific understanding. They would do well to conclude, as we could, that it shows a good mastery of some of the important implicit rules for the satisfactory completion of worksheets.

What we seem to have discovered so far in this chapter is that success in science appears to have a lot more to do with understanding the cognitive and communicative rules that are operating in the classroom environment, rather than being dependent on the use of 'scientific' language. So now, to pursue the point further, let us look at some situations where pupils have been given the opportunity to use 'non-scientific' styles of writing, and see how this affects their achievement.

Widening the range of writing in science

We have seen in the previous section that many of the arguments for restricting children's writing in science to the formal report do not in fact stand up to close scrutiny. However, many science teachers are reluctant to allow children to use other forms of writing because they have had experience of children producing pieces of work that lacked the qualities of scientific thinking that they are trying to encourage. We therefore need to explore some of the problems in this area. We have chosen to concentrate on types of imaginative or 'creative' writing that lie in direct contrast to the report format, in the hope that some of the issues are more clearly identifiable through such a juxtaposition. But we expect our conclusions to hold good for any more informal writing genre that might be used in the subject.

The work of the upper-stream boy identified as Philip

(i) Worksheet (Philip's writing in italics)

Photosynthesis

1 Using a cork borer, cut discs from a leaf which has been in the light for several hours.

Drop these discs into a beaker of boiling water. Leave for two minutes in order to kill the cells.

Make sure all bunsen burners are out.

Remove the discs and put them into a test-tube ¼ full of alcohol.

Heat in a water bath for three minutes.

2 What happens to the alcohol — *The alcohol went a dark greenish colour*

3 What happens to the colour of the discs — *The discs went a white colour*

4 What has the alcohol done to the discs — *The alcohol has removed the chlorophyl*

5 Pour off the alcohol into the container provided, and rinse them in water to soften them

Place the discs on a white tile and cover with drops of iodine

6 For what substances are you testing — *Starch*

7 What colour are the discs — *The discs turned black*

8 Repeat steps 1 and 5, using discs cut from a leaf which has been in darkness for two days

9 What does the iodine test show in these discs — *The iodine shows that in the discs there is no starch in the leaf*

10 What do you think the role of light is with green leaves — *Light is needed for the formation of starch in the leaf*

(ii) Continuous writing

What happens to air when a Candle burns in it

When a candle is burning in air it keeps lit until the candle goes out. This is because the oxygen in a jar is used to help burn things such as candles. One of the experiments that shows this is you get a trough and a jar and a candle with a cork holding it vertically up and supporting it. Then you get some water filled into the trough and the jar should be put in the trough with the candle floating inside the jar.

(diagram)

After a while the candle should have rised. This is because the heat given from the candle goes to the water out and pushed in the jar.

Figure 2.3 Worksheet answers and continuous writing
This pupil's answers show awareness of the ground rules for worksheets
(Example taken from Wade and Wood, 1979, pp. 133–5)

What happens when science teachers allow children to use more imaginative or creative writing in their lessons? If we look at some examples where children have responded in different ways to these kind of tasks, we can see if there are dangers, as far as the development of their scientific thinking is concerned, or indeed, if there might not be positive advantages in the setting of this type of task on occasions. Figures 2.4 and 2.5 show the originals of two pieces of writing where children, having spent some time looking at insect life, were given the opportunity to write about what they had learned. They were told that, if they wished, they could write about the life of a spider from the spider's point of view. Only five pupils chose to take up this offer, and these two pupils produced the most detailed stories. Because the originals are not easy to read, here are the 'translations' with spelling and punctuation amended where necessary, to make the meaning clear:

Example 1: *Life as a Spider*

As I woke up I saw my house reduced by some big fool who is known as a human. They call us spiders. We have 8 segmental legs which means which are in joints. Ho! Well I have to build my house again. My house is in a tree where I build my house using silk. My house is a food net which chases food. It is sticky so any fly come by, if it does not see my web it would crash in to the [net] and get stuck. Then I come along and wrap the fly up in my silk like a cocoon so it stays nice and cool. When I am hungry I eat the fly. Our worst enemy is the bird which we are the best food for them. I have to go now because here comes a bird. Bye! Thank goodness he's gone. I live in the middle of the web because if any insect hits the web I can feel it and get him before he gets away. Oh! no, he's come back.

Example 2: *Tarantula*

It was early Sunday morning. I was under a tree. I looked at myself. I had 8 legs and hairs all over my body. I knew what I had transformed into as soon as I looked at my mouth. I was a tarantula. I looked up: all I could see was a load of feet so I climbed up a woman's leg. She saw me and panicked so I bit her. About 5 minutes later a policeman started to try to squash [swat?] me so I bit him. After that I was tired and hungry so I got something to eat. I was walking for a long time before I found out where my legs were taking me, I was in the South American desert. I was lost for good unless my legs will take me to the city.

I looked all around me. I couldn't see anything except pieces of sand. I tried to eat some sand but it got stuck in my mouth. After I got over my sore mouth I found a little spider so I ate it. It tasted nice to me so I ate another and another until I was full. When I got full I felt like going to sleep. While I was asleep I had a dream that I was asleep in my bedroom in Bradford, England.

That next morning I woke up. I was in my bed at home. My mum said I was having a bad dream so she woke me up. I overheard the news saying a Tarantula was loose in London after getting out of the zoo. The two people it stung were in hospital, in stable condition.

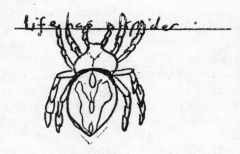

Life as a spider

Has I worked up I saw my house reched
by some big food to who is known as a
human. They call use spiders we have
8 segmental legs which means which one in
joints. Ho! well I have to build
my house agian. My house is in a tree
were I build my house using silk.
My house is a food
net which chages
food. It is sticki so
any fly come hang if
it does not see my
web it would crash
in to the and get chuk. Then I
come along and lap the fly up in

Figure 2.4 Life as a spider
A good attempt at using the ground rules for imaginative writing in science

Readers might like to consider their own initial reactions to these stories:

- Which one do you prefer and why?
- How much scientific knowledge are the children communicating?
- Do you think this is a valid writing exercise to set?

my ~~stik~~ silk like a ~~cocoon~~ ↑ cocoon ~~t~~ so it strays
nice and ~~g~~ cool ; when I am hungry I
eat the ~~fly~~ flie . Our ~~most~~ enemie is the
bird which we are the ~~~~ best good for
them . I have t go know because here
comes a bird, big! Thank good ness he's
gon . I live in the ~~middle~~ middle of the
web because if any ~~g~~ insect hits the web
I can ~~speak~~ it and get him before he gds away
oh! know he's come ~~by~~ back.

Notice the different ways in which the pupils have approached the task. In the first example, we are given an enthusiastic but essentially down-to-earth and realistic account of the activities of a spider, with some detailed information about its bodily structure and how it goes about catching its prey (together with accompanying diagrams). In the second example, we have a tremendous adventure story about that most notorious of spiders, the tarantula. The action takes us from South America to Bradford to London, and two people are severely injured. Finally, the writer has to devote considerable space to explaining away the fantasy, by using the cliche of it all being a dream.

How can we explain these different conceptualizations of the task? Let us consider the different frameworks the pupils brought to it. The second pupil was not normally a good worker in science lessons. However, he took to this task immediately, and worked solidly and in silence until he had completed it, 15 minutes later. But what he was able to write was hampered by the fact that he had not actually learned much about spiders, and therefore he did not have a fund of knowledge to work from, unlike the first pupil. However, out of school he had learned about tarantulas, and he also listened to a brief comment about them in the class. He was interested in the idea of evil spiders, particularly when they climb up women's legs. He also knew, from everyday life, and his English lessons, how to write a 'ripping yarn'. So he transformed the task into one which he enjoyed and could do. The effect of this task, therefore, had been to motivate a reluctant learner, but it had not significantly enhanced or displayed his scientific understanding. Whether it makes him take a keener interest in future science

Taranchaler.   19th of May 1988

it was early sunday morning I was
under a tree, I looked at myself
I had 8 legs and hares all over
myself body. I new what I had
transformed into as soon as I looked
at my mouth, I was a taranchaler.
I Looked up, all I could see
was a load of feet so I climed
up a womans leg. she saw
me and paniced so I bit her.
about 5 minutes later a police
man Started to try to
squatt me so I bit him
after that I Was tired and
hungry So I got something to
eat. I was walking for a long
time bethore I found out ware
my legs were taking me, I
was in the South American
desert. I was lost for good unles
my legs will take me to the

city.
I looked all around me I couldent
see aneything accept prices of sand.
I tried to eat some sand but

it got stuck in my mouth.
after I got over my saw mouth
I found a little spider
so I ate it.
it tasted nice to me so
I ate another and another until I was full
when I got full I felt
like going to sleep.
while I was asleep I had
a dream that I was asleep
in my bedroom in Bradford
england.
that next morning I woke
up I was in my bed at
home my mum' said I
was having a bad dream
so she woke me up. I overheard
the news saying I
taranchaler was loose in
london after getting
out of the Zoo. the
two people it stung were
in hospital, instable condition.

Figure 2.5 Tarantula
An exciting read, but this writing fails to employ essential ground rules about conveying
scientific knowledge

lessons, as a result of his 'success' in this one, is a matter for debate. So the task was useful in some ways, but not in others.

The first pupil's work must be judged more effective from the point of view of science teaching, and can be explained by the fact that this pupil has a great interest in natural history, was more involved in the lesson content, and was thus able to surround the task with a different framework of rules for its completion. He was also well aware of his audience, the *science* teacher, and the desirability of displaying his knowledge. He came to the work with different needs and purposes, and with a different background of experiences from which to select his rules for completing the task.

We can only explain their different performances through a fairly intimate knowledge of their background orientation to school and to the subject, and their degree of motivation in this particular lesson. However, nonscientific interpretations of the task are not confined to reluctant learners. The chapter on writing in the humanities shows how some of the most well-intentioned pupils can also make similar miscalculations or deliberate misinterpretations in connection with their work. Obviously, if science teachers are going to set this kind of work, and have an interest in children displaying the degree of their scientific learning, then the rules surrounding the task have to be made more explicit, in some way, if it is to serve the purpose they intend.

Other types of imaginative work in science may not be prone to such difficulties of interpretation, as they are more tightly framed. In the following example, the pupils were told to imagine they had shrunk to an incredibly small size, and were journeying through the solid, liquid and gaseous states of a substance, at the molecular level:

Journey into solid, liquid and gas

I was picked to go on a journey, and for the journey I had to be shrunk to a size small enough to fit in [between?] the particle of a solid, liquid or gas. I had been shrunk and was ready to set off into a solid. As soon as I was in the solid I noticed that the ground and everything around me was shaking. I was surrounded by particles that were close together and it was like a maze in between them. As I walked I heard the sound of the particles vibrating.

I returned to the surface and was put in a liquid. The particles were further apart and they moved more randomly. The particles moved about in clusters, breaking apart sometimes. I saw a gap between the particles and headed for it, but before I got there the gap was taken by another particle.

I was then put in a gas. As I entered the gas I saw that there was hardly any particles. The particles moved about quickly. I was nearly hit by a particle as it moved past. Another particle came and this time I was hit. It had broke my arm so I decided to get out before another came.

In this example, the imaginative mode tests the child's concepts of solid, liquid and gaseous states, but is not a particularly good example of imaginative prose. The next script is a small extract from a pupil with greater enthusiasm in her use of language and an equal grasp of the concepts. (For those science teachers who might have reservations about teaching about molecular structure in these concrete terms, rather than emphasizing the fact that they are models, there is additional interest in considering these examples.)

> '. . . I'm in the solid state and oh boy is this bouncy, it's all wobbly and there is a low noise, a sort of buzz. The particles are so close together I can walk from one to another and if I fall I just bounce back together! onto another particle. There is a low humming noise all around me of which I have never heard before . . .

Both examples include the same sort of information that we would encounter in a formal impersonal account, but the imaginative style may actually help to clarify the extent to which the pupils understand, perhaps by encouraging them into giving a more detailed account, or by testing their interpretation through pushing their imagination further. Thus, there seems little doubt that tasks like these can, on occasion, both significantly enhance pupils' understanding and allow the teacher to make an accurate assessment of it. Let us not be over-confident, however. Some pupils always make mistakes and here is one who doesn't realize just how small he's supposed to be. As a result, he's being imaginative by showing us he understands what polystyrene looks like when you're very small, but we don't find out about his conceptual grasp of the solid state:

> As I beamed myself down into the solid to explore what it was like inside I experienced a most frightening shock, I found myself with little room to move in. I had to find a way out. I didn't know where to go in this black hole as I was somewhere in the middle of the polystyrene. I climbed up a few of the strange round bubbles only to find myself slipping down a couple until I eventually hit the bottom with a thud. I got out my battery operated drill and drilled a hole . . .

Other imaginative tasks allow pupils to operate at a higher cognitive level. Figure 2.6 is an example quoted by Sutton (1981, p. 16), where a girl is required to show her grasp of the molecular structure of a liquid by comparing it with the behaviour of a football crowd.

The samples quoted help us to appreciate both the potentialities and problems of setting imaginative tasks in science. Obviously, they need not be additional 'fripperies' – 'creative stories' lacking a scientific perspective, and sidetracking children from the real business of science. On the contrary, carefully chosen alternatives to the scientific report can excite children's interest and test their conceptual grasp. We simply need to be aware of what can go wrong and why, rather than dismissing the whole enterprise, or relegating it to the occasional poetry-writing exercise in the end-of-term chemistry lesson!

In the light of this whole discussion of teachers' fears and our examples of children's work and thinking, we can now make some appraisal of the fundamental controversy about writing in science to which we referred briefly at the start of this chapter.

Why is a liquid like, or not like, a football crowd.

First of all, the kinetic theory suggests that all matter is made up of tiny particles called molecules, which are always in continuous motion. Fans, off course, are always like this, all being small bits of one big crowd and they never stay still at a game.

Also, liquids take the shape of their container; put a football crowd in a hexagnal stand, and they will take on that shape.

When the liquids temperature is increased, the particles vibrate even more fiercely and eventually those eratic movements overcome the internal attractive forces and the particles in the liquid break away i.e. the liquid boils likewise. When trouble begins to bubble at a match, the fans blood begins to boil and they start to move about even more. ~~Finally, they~~ Eventually, they break away and spill out onto the pitch.

However, on cooling, the particles slow down and come back to their principle state. The same thing happens at the match, when the trouble dies down, the fans go back to their seats.

Figure 2.6 Why is a liquid like, or not like, a football crowd
A pupil uses her imagination strictly within the scientific perspective
(Example taken from Sutton, 1981, p. 16)

In Chapter 1, we discussed James Britton's progressive ideas about the kind of writing children needed to do in order to learn more effectively in specialist subjects. His recommendations began to reach a wide audience of teachers after the publication of the Bullock Report, *A Language for Life* (DES, 1975), although he and like-minded others had developed their views during the mid to late 1960s. Britton suggests that writing can be divided into three main categories: expressive, transactional and poetic. Transactional language was the kind of writing Britton found being used in most specialist subject areas other than English. He suggested that there were many sub-categories of trans-actional prose, including the scientific report, and provided a succinct definition of its major characteristics:

> This is the language to get things done: to inform people (telling them what they need or want to know or what we think they ought to know), to advise or persuade or instruct people. Thus the transactional is used for example to record facts, exchange opinions, explain and explore ideas, construct theories; to transact business, conduct campaigns, change public opinion. (Britton *et al.*, 1975, p. 88)

Britton suggests that expressive writing is 'closest' to the child, as it re-sembles natural speech. As the child grew intellectually, Britton argued, he would naturally come to terms with the other two principal forms of written language, but in the early stages of learning in science, or any subject for that matter, it was beneficial if the child could use language that came naturally to him, rather than being forced into the transactional mould. Britton also insisted that the process of writing expressively could actively assist learning; he called this 'writing to learn'. Britton found his analysis of the types of writing being done in secondary school subjects profoundly disappointing, because he was committed to the view that expressive language was an aid to effective learning, and yet it was being neglected by teachers, especially in the sciences. Similar findings were noted by Spencer (1983) in his survey of Scottish schools, and across the Atlantic in the USA the pattern was also similar.

Most of this research and the progressive theories that accompanied it were the work of teachers of English, and during the late 1970s there was some vituperative criticism of it, with writers mainly commenting on the fact that Britton and his supporters were emphasizing the personal emotional growth of pupils at the expense of their intellectual development in scientific thinking. The best example of such criticism is contained in a small book by Jeanette Williams (1977) entitled *Learning to Write or Writing to Learn*. She expresses concern that adopting Britton's views on language and learning would in fact deny children access to the distinctive perceptions of specialist subjects. Her argument rests on her view that each specialist subject has its own form of thought that can only find expression through the particular specialist language which is characteristic of it. She suggested that unless children were en-couraged to operate within the language of specialist subjects from the start, it would be impossible for them to employ the appropriate frames of reference for thinking in those subjects.

In Williams's argument, her use of the term 'language' is probably best defined as 'a way of seeing' into which the learner is initiated by specialist teachers. Williams believed that without the help and guidance of specialist teachers, and with too much emphasis on expressive language and self-directed learning, children are likely to be trapped within 'common sense language' and 'undisciplined' modes of thinking (a view also shared by Richards, some of whose work we quoted earlier). Put crudely, Williams, and others who share her view, see scientific concepts percolating down into the child's consciousness from a fount of publicly established 'disciplined thinking' and specialist language. By contrast, writers like Britton tend to think that such concepts will develop 'naturally', growing out of the child's experience, and capable of being expressed in everyday language. Williams (1977, p. 47) is highly critical of Britton's approach:

> In advocating more use of the 'expressive' throughout the curriculum, it [Britton's team] is in a sense imprisoning the child in a web of common-sense concepts . . .

In his reply to her criticisms, Britton *et al.* (1979) shows that he is aware that there are two different views of knowledge. The first is that espoused by writers like Williams and Richards, who see subject knowledge as 'a public domain' – an established set of rules and practices, with a distinctive philosophical base. The task of the subject teacher is to 'socialize' the new learner into its rules and practices. The second view of knowledge is that it is 'an individual construction'. Here the emphasis is on the process the learner goes through as he constructs new meanings for himself. Britton recognizes that these differing definitions should not really lie in opposition to each other. But a lot of the Language Across the Curriculum literature, which Britton's work gave rise to, does seem to emphasize personal growth and self-discovery, rather than showing awareness of the structural elements of knowledge – the frameworks of rules that comprise disciplined ways of thinking.

Williams's point that there are 'common sense' ways of seeing things and that these can be contrasted with specialist subject ways of seeing things, is at the heart of the debate, and has also been an issue that we have addressed throughout this chapter. However, our analysis of children's writing has suggested that perhaps the issue of a scientific perspective is a little more complex than Williams seems to think. If we wish to take the debate further, we need to incorporate these new insights into the argument, and see how they relate to what both sides are suggesting.

Let us first make the assumption, based on our evidence, that, in school, specialist subjects consist of collections of both implicit and explicit rules and 'organizing principles' governing both academic cognition and the communication of knowledge in writing. Within the science classroom we expect children to perform a variety of cognitive and communicative tasks, each with their own particular sets of ground rules or framework. It then becomes unrealistic to conceive of a 'subject perspective' as a single, coherent and unproblematic frame of reference. At whatever level, a specialist subject label must be an 'umbrella' term for all these different rules and frameworks. And if there is such a collection of different frames in each subject, then this must also be true of what is so often simply referred to as 'commonsense knowledge'. Thus the simple distinction between the 'everyday' and the 'specialist' knowledge, which Britton and Williams (and many other writers in different fields) make, may mask the number and the heterogeneity of the various collections of ground rules and frameworks within both categories.

Williams keeps emphasizing the importance of specialist language in science, but the more she discusses it the more she seems to be using it as a way of describing the interpretive frameworks used in the disciplines. If we accept that cognitive and communicative ground rules are the essential definers of any discipline, then surely one can, if one wishes, allow the use of any of three language forms identified by Britton. There can be nothing intrinsically wrong with allowing pupils to express their personal identity, imagination, enthusiasms and values in their writing in science. The only danger would be if we accepted such expressions as a *substitute* for 'disciplined' thinking, and concentrated on them to the exclusion of the different frames of reference that the disciplines encourage us to develop. It is true that, at the higher levels, public scientific debate is conventionally couched in impersonal 'transactional' language, but that does not make it an inevitable or necessary part of scientific learning in school. Williams and her sympathizers confuse the appearance (impersonal language and technical jargon) with the substance – the cognitive frames within which the teachers and, we hope, the pupils are operating.

But neither need there be the extreme reluctance that Britton evinces to use impersonal language. Williams is undoubtedly right when she criticizes his team for allowing the concerns of English teachers to predominate, at the expense of the subject teachers' concerns about content, and time constraints. As she says:

> With a curious lack of imagination, they approached writing in all subjects as though it were writing in English, forgetting, or ignoring, the fact that for the English teacher, kinds of writing are part of the actual subject-matter of the discipline, whereas for other teachers writing is a means only. (Williams, 1977, p. 39)

If part of the process of teaching in science involves uncovering and communicating ground rules and frameworks then perhaps a more sensitive and flexible approach to the selection of writing tasks and styles is what is really needed. There may be positive value on some occasions in presenting children with models of scientific prose and setting them tasks where they have to write in similar vein, especially with secondary age pupils whose work we have been considering in this chapter. For until external examiners accept a wider range of writing styles in the scripts they mark, children will need to know the ground rules of the examination game. But, on other occasions, or with pupils who do not take easily to the style, teaching strategies using expressive or even poetic modes may achieve the teacher's objectives, if chosen with understanding and sensitivity. Critical discussion of different genres might encourage pupils to become aware of some of the different frameworks that writers conventionally operate in. It also provides them with the opportunity to make more reflective and positive choices about how they will write themselves.

Obviously, the real priority is to have a skilled specialist subject teacher who can provide children with the learning environment they need in order to move into the ways of thinking that are characteristic of the discipline. What the 'framework theory' we have elaborated in this book can provide, is the opportunity for teachers to reject the polarized and dogmatic views of both the 'traditionalists' and the 'progressives' over the issue of writing in science. Once we understand the problem more clearly, we can begin to see some possible solutions.

3 Writing in the humanities

It is best to begin a chapter on the humanities with some definition of the subjects under consideration. In many schools, a Humanities Faculty is large, embracing English and religious education, as well as history, geography, various social sciences, and any number of integrated courses. In other schools, it may be a smaller department, perhaps dealing with only history, geography and social studies. Because in this book writing in English is considered in a separate chapter, we deal here with writing in connection with all the other above-mentioned subject areas and, in the light of the National Curriculum, focus our attention particularly on the compulsory foundation subjects of history and geography.

In the past decade or so, the kind of written work expected from pupils in these areas has begun to undergo a transformation as a result of two main influences. One of these has been the Language Across the Curriculum movement and associated progressive pedagogies that placed a new importance on the role of writing for the development of pupils' learning. Teachers were advised to set a wider variety of writing tasks, to encourage more subjective and expressive written responses, and to devise more issues-based or pupil-centred courses to improve pupils' motivation to learn by providing the opportunity for more relevant and practical written work. More recently, the advent of the new GCSE examinations has resulted in the work of older secondary pupils also taking on a new character, when in both examination and coursework elements they may be asked to display their learning in a variety of writing styles demanding a high level of competence. These include, for instance, lengthy accounts of fieldwork projects, extended essays, simulated newspaper reports and articles, written drafts of speeches and even documentary-style dialogues and interviews, as well as the more traditional paragraph or short essay answer.

Unfortunately, both pressure of time and a belief in 'natural flair' mean that many subject teachers seriously neglect the teaching of these necessary writing skills. Others, working within their own subject area, imagine that such skills are being adequately taught in English lessons, yet there is little evidence in many schools that teachers are engaged in the extensive interdepartmental liaison required for this to be effectively the case. In this chapter, we try to show the need for changed attitudes and new teaching strategies in order to remedy such a state of affairs, for unless we do something about it, systems of examination and assessment in the humanities will continue to favour the already competent and seriously disadvantage many others. However, it would require another book to do justice to this comprehensively, so we begin by being very selective, and only drawing attention to some of the competences required. We do this to focus particular attention on areas that are frequently neglected by teachers because they tend to be 'hidden', often as a result of being taken-for-granted. The chapter begins by looking at the skills of note-taking and answering various types of assessment question. This includes, as in Chapter 2, some discussion of the way our analysis of children's writing in humanities subjects can shed some light on the nature of 'disciplined' thinking. Finally, we consider a current controversy in the area of history teaching, i.e. the 'empathy question'; not because we share any particular partiality for this discipline, but because it provides a good example of how the 'ground rules' theory we have employed throughout this book can be used to sharpen and clarify understanding of children's writing and learning, and help with the development of more effective teaching techniques.

Taking notes

Taking notes is a common tradition in many subject areas, but perhaps none more so than the humanities, where it is the equivalent of the scientific report format we found in the sciences. None the less, even in the most modern classroom, note-taking is a basic skill that children need to acquire. Many teacher education manuals, while providing plenty of ideas relating to lessons, neglect the rather boring and seemingly old-fashioned task of getting pupils to make clear notes that are to be used as a permanent record, despite the fact that practising teachers spend a lot of time (far too much according to official reports) trying to get pupils to do this. We have yet to see, for example, a debate on the relative merits of photocopied sheets versus dictated notes and yet the use of both is common practice. While we can be certain that children will learn most through active participation in well-thought-out and stimulating activities, and that skills are the result of practice, teachers and examinations still demand a certain amount of tested 'knowledge and understanding' as the literature on learning objectives usually phrases it. This means that children must have a well-organized file or book to refer to, which summarizes what they have learned. Many teachers believe that dictation is a time-consuming, boring and not very effective method of note-taking, and pupils are set various other types of written task to achieve the same end. We therefore need to examine what is typically set to produce pupils' own written record of learning, and with what effect. While study skills manuals on note-taking concentrate mainly on teaching the mechanics of the task, we concentrate here on pupils' understanding of what they are doing and the problems they may encounter.

Sometimes notes may be made in the preliminary stages of coursework assignments, often as a background to practical investigations or as a preparation for essay work. Alternatively, notes may be written as a summary of work already 'done', perhaps through discussion or as part of a group work exercise. In this context, they are then often kept as an important reference material for revision and examination work. In both cases, they may be characterized as types of 'personal' writing, because they will not be presented as the finished product of the pupil's learning or used for formal assessment. Instead, the pupils' learning will be presented in another form: an examination answer, an essay or a piece of project work. But, for a number of reasons, the notes produced by pupils often differ from those produced by adult learners. School surveys (DES, 1975; Spencer, 1983) suggest that either for reasons of conservatism, class control or financial stringency, children spend a lot of their time in the classroom laboriously recording information in their books or on file paper, and often copying considerable chunks of textbook prose. For the moment, we shall therefore consider some of the routines of note-taking that are common in secondary schools.

Teachers each tend to have their own rules about note-taking, so that rather than acquiring their own note-taking style, children have to learn the different rules that apply in their various lessons. In our own survey, pupils commented, for example, on the differences between the various types of notes they were expected to take in different lessons, either dictated, copied, or summaries produced by the pupils themselves. They also commented on the distinction between notes that were written in jotters and those that were copied up or written in 'best' books. The type of notes taken by pupils was usually determined by the teacher, thus giving the pupil little choice about style or purpose, and turning note-taking into an unthinking classroom routine, rather than a variable and meaningful activity. The main requirement was to know what each teacher expected:

> Teachers have their own meaning for the phrase take notes. Taking notes in jotters usually means taking notes in shorthand manner but in books it can mean roughly or neatly depending on the teacher and you have to get to know the individual teacher to know what they mean.

One girl even showed how 'notes' was, in fact, a shorthand term used by teachers to describe the *quantity* of writing required in an account:

> If it is in your book they mean they don't want a long piece of work, but if you put notes like: 'Harold fought William, William won, he was made King', which are notes they give you a low mark and tell you to re-write it. So I think they want a middle length descriptive account.

In addition, our research revealed some interesting information about the difficulties that some pupils face when insufficient attention is paid to helping children to develop this skill. Note-taking may appear to be a simple matter to adult subject teachers who are highly competent in this area, but in fact children have to be sensitive to a number of factors in order to perform this task satisfactorily. Most pupils were aware that notes should be short and simple and only include important points of information. However, a number of pupils only mentioned the 'surface' criteria of leaving out words and shortening sentences, without mentioning the idea of homing in on the key ideas in a text:

> When teachers ask you to take notes they mean write about the subject you are doing, but not in long sentences. Writing in notes means you can miss out words like and, they, the, was, went, etc. This is so it explains things easily for you to understand but quicker to write.

Such pupils saw note-taking as a way of compressing *all* the information presented. This technique was also consciously preferred by some pupils as a way of resolving their problem of what to include and what to leave out. Such pupils doubted their own capacity to discriminate between important and relatively unimportant information. Such a strategy was both easier work intellectually, and certain to count as successful completion of the task. Fundamentally, however, it resulted from the fact that they did not share the teacher's construction of what was relevant to the particular task in hand. Knowing what is relevant when only the teacher has a full understanding of the objective of the lesson, or when you are embarking on some vast uncharted sea-voyage of project work, is indeed a problem. It is a problem because you don't know the framework: you haven't got the teacher's conceptualization of the task. We recommend, therefore, that subject teachers begin to see it as part of their task to communicate those ground rules and try out methods designed to signal or advertise some of the parameters. Note-taking doesn't make sense unless pupils have some wider contextual map of the task. The problem, of course, is similar to the one we encountered in Chapter 2, where teachers asked pupils only to include the 'important' points relating to their experiments.

Faced with such difficulties as this, pupils, for reasons of insecurity, unfamiliarity or lack of motivation, may grasp at anything that offers them an easy way out. For instance, some pupils were set an assignment on the history and future development of the local transport network and two pupils were later found desperately and laboriously copying out details of the building of the Bridgewater canal, a remote distance from their home town. This was despite clear general written and oral instructions. It was only after the teacher spent considerable time with these pupils, where the framework of the task was discussed at length with them individually, that they had the ability and confidence to use material selectively, sifting it for relevant information, and distinguishing what they needed for a brief overview of the development of canals in Britain, to put in context the information they had found out about the local canal. There do not appear to be any easy answers to this kind of problem, especially when it is compounded by having large classes of pupils doing individual assignments. But it is one which we need to recognize and work on, so that children progress from producing low-level 'scrap-book' assignments to producing meaningful and coherent pieces of work. Brainstorming sessions to produce hypotheses or simply just questions, to direct the child's enquiry, can provide a useful focus, as can planning a campaign of action to follow to find some of the answers. Such activities help to focus pupils' minds on the kind of issues we have been discussing. Any experienced teacher is, however, only too aware of children's preference for plunging rather than planning, as well as the fact that individual children vary in the ways they begin to work on topics. But knowing why children tend to react in the way described above provides both the comfort of explanation for the pupils' difficulties and a starting point for experimenting with teaching techniques that will offer more help.

Where notes are used to record learning for some future examination, then the teacher has often already structured the learning in a sequence of lessons, perhaps involving discussion, simulations, group activities of various kinds and audio-visual material. Pupils are not always asked to write extensively. Some teachers provide a printed alternative to a set of dictated notes, e.g. reminders of 'What You Have Learned in this Unit' to which the children can add. These are useful to some children, but are limited in the sense that they do not actively engage the pupils, and are too often simply set aside. Alternative materials include revision sheets with gaps to be filled in, or any one of a host of similar exercises. Unfortunately, children's usual response to filling gaps is to turn the exercise into a race to the finish, where understanding comes a poor second to the satisfaction of a completed sheet.

Despite these commonly used techniques, however, there are many times when note-taking involves pupils in lengthy written work. Many teachers guide pupils through this by providing a series of questions to be answered on whatever work has been covered in class, or on reading from a textbook. In our survey, the teachers said this had three main virtues: children of all abilities could cope with the task, provided that questions are appropriately graded; it provides a useful test of understanding; and it is a handy revision aid. The teachers usually demanded that the pupils write their answers in 'full sentences' and again this was classroom shorthand for 'make sure you rearrange the words in the question to start off your answer'. For example:

Q: What are some of the main reasons for the high infant mortality rate in the third world?

A: Some of the main reasons for the high infant mortality rate in the third world are . . .

Such a format meant that teachers did not have to refer to question sheets when checking work, while pupils, given a logically set-out sheet of questions, had a clear and unambiguous account of whatever topic they had studied, provided they got the answers right.

Unfortunately, there are some drawbacks to this seemingly effective method. If pupils answer a series of graded questions using 'full sentences', the account that results is a piece of writing that usually has the appearance of order and understanding. However, because of the mechanical way in which such tasks are completed, such a strategy may in fact be of only limited usefulness in helping pupils to become more autonomous in their ability to write coherent notes. The contrast between the ease with which such pre-structured writing was completed, and the greater difficulties that pupils face when given no help in structuring their work, was apparent in our survey. What such techniques did produce were maximum tangible results in terms of *apparent* achievement. Using such techniques, a pupil whose understanding of a topic was quite limited could be 'led through it' and produce an amount of what appeared to be organized and intelligent work. Thus the output and success of the lesson seemed greater than it actually was. This is a point that is also important when considering the use of structured and unstructured questions for assessment, and we shall return to it later.

There are many less common, but probably equally useful, additional ways of recording information for future reference. Pupils can work effectively individually or in pairs to prepare their own summaries, rearrange sentences or paragraphs provided by the teacher, or engage in any of a host of practical activities that will provide a lasting record of what they need to remember. The best of these will be well-integrated into the main body of coursework, as the natural outcome of it. In this way, the task of note-taking becomes a meaningful one, where pupils relate to their learning, instead of unthinkingly recording material, from which they will then find it more difficult to revise for examinations.

It is in this context that many writers who are sympathetic to the idea that pupils should be able to use expressive language in their work, have suggested that learning can be enhanced if pupils are allowed to reflect on their learning in their written record, by including their own personal reactions and comments, or perhaps keeping some sort of diary in parallel with their more formal note-taking, by using for example the left-hand or right-hand side pages of a book exclusively for each. (Some teachers, on the other hand, express doubts about the advisability of this, claiming that by concentrating on personal issues and not using the formal language of the subject they are studying, children fail to develop a 'disciplined' perspective. Their concerns are the same as those of the science teachers in Chapter 2, and we address this issue once again in the next section of this chapter, in connection with assessment answers.) However, one of the major functions of such informal 'expressive' writing is to provide the teacher with feedback about the pupil's progress. Under such circumstances, it is hardly 'natural' writing, but is as much of a display of genre learning as any other form.

As such there are, as ever, ground rules to follow and decisions to make about what is appropriate to include or leave out.

Assessment answers

In this section, we deal with various forms of writing that are commonly set by teachers and examiners in the course of routine class assessment of varying degrees of formality, as well as external examinations. As we commented at the start of this chapter, many different styles of writing may be demanded. In addition, one important thing to consider is the length of continuous prose that children are expected to produce. This may vary from the short single sentence answer to sustained writing of two or three pages in length for some examinations, and much longer pieces of work for assessed coursework.

It is not our intention to provide a handbook of tips for teaching the stylistic niceties of the wide range of diaries, speeches, letters, essays and projects that are now commonplace as the formats for written work. Instead, our main theme through the rest of this chapter is that in order to perform successfully, pupils have to become adept at reading the mind of the assessor, as many important instructions are left unspoken. Pupils who get the answers right are those who have been able to work out for themselves what the ground rules for the task are or, more usually, they have almost intuitively absorbed those rules.

Shorter structured questions

A clear example of implicit rules in short answer questions is provided by Hull (1985). He describes how an examination question was being discussed by a group of history teachers. The pupils were expected to fill in the missing word in the sentence 'A Norman castle would be a _____ source of evidence.' The right answer was 'primary'. Hull inquired if a child who put 'interesting' would be given a mark. The teachers rejected this as a possibility, and explained that the children had already been primed to give the right answer, because all the previous teaching had revolved around the concepts of primary and secondary sources of evidence. In this case, then, the pupils had to be careful to make sure that their answer related to the focus in the previous lesson – the identification of primary and secondary sources of evidence. Any pupil who misread the ground rules for this question may simply have thought that it centred on Norman castles, which of course it did not.

Other questions require knowledge of ground rules concerning length and detail. Here are two answers to a question about pollution from sewage, carrying two marks:

Sewage disposal can be a huge problem if not dealt with correctly. The sewage from homes and factories does go through sewage plants where it is treated, but unfortunately this is often not enough and some raw sewage does get into rivers where it pollutes them and kills off living things. Seaside towns sometimes just let their sewage just flow down long pipes and into the sea untreated, where it is brought back into the beaches by the tide and makes the beaches dirty and a health hazard.

Sewage is being poured into lakes and rivers which is also costing money to get cleaned up so that we can drink the water and swim in it without affecting our health in any way.

The second pupil seems to know less, but perhaps only lacks the ability to think reflexively about the knowledge she has and how to display it. Most teachers would agree that the first answer is well worth two marks, but you might like to reflect on how you would mark the second one.

An even more disturbing example is provided by a specimen GCSE sociology paper from the Midland Examining Group. Here a considerable number of marks are available, but no clues are given about the length of answer required, or what sort of information is being demanded. The question below is the first in a series on stimulus material:

(The stimulus
Pupils were shown reproductions of the front pages and lead stories in Argentinian and British tabloid newspapers published during the Falklands War.)

The question
Compare the content of the Argentinian and British newspaper reports. What major differences and similarities do you notice in the layout and content of the newspapers? (8 marks)

The question provides only a very brief guide about how to tackle the task. It is left to the pupil to create the ground rules for answering it. A well-taught pupil will identify first that it is worth eight marks, so a couple of sentences obviously will not do. They may also work out that at least two similarities and differences should be mentioned. However, the true extent of the ground rules is only revealed in the mark scheme, which remains secret to the examiners:

The mark scheme
Level 1: A valid similarity and difference between a face value. (1–2 marks)
Level 2: A general synthesis of the differences and similarities between sources. A statement about the differences in approach between the Argentinian emphasis on character assassination and the British emphasis on patriotism and 'good news'. (3–5 marks)
Level 3: Precise and balanced statements based on direct reference to sources showing an understanding of the purposes of both sides in the media war and the *different* aims of the press coverage. (6–8 marks)

The pupil is working in the dark, and an extensive decoding operation is necessary to get close to the rules for a level 3 answer. While the examiners believe they are testing understanding and concept development, they are in reality relying, for their better answers, on pupils having a sophisticated awareness of the style of answer that is required: abstract generalization rather than concrete example; reasons for the differences rather than simply descriptions of them; academic language, and so on. Though the paper was designed in theory for a broad cross-section of the school population, it is unlikely that they could all cope successfully with this question even if they all knew the answers. It is typical of a genre of question where the highest marks are reserved for those who are acutely sensitive to, and well practised in, the rules of the examination game, and can think along the same lines as the examiners, decoding what is really required and correctly resolving any ambiguities. When pupils were asked to complete this question as a classwork assessment, many more able pupils provided only relatively short answers that were far from comprehensive, whereas when they were interviewed later, with more questions to guide them, their answers revealed a much greater depth of knowledge.

In our survey, many pupils were well aware that if a teacher asked for a paragraph answer they were really asking for an answer of a certain length, while the more sophisticated thinkers were also aware that the answer would usually be a short in-depth account on one subject. Again, as with note-taking, there were those pupils who concentrated on the surface criteria of indentation and length, whereas others related the format to content – the need for depth and confinement to a single subject – thus revealing a deeper understanding. Provided they were given the cue-word 'paragraph', the pupils knew what was expected of them. The problem for some of the less able was to actually write sustained prose.

The above examples also help us to return to the point we raised earlier, in relation to notes, about structuring a series of questions to draw out what the pupil knows. In the question above, pupils need to write at least, say, half a page to a page of connected prose in order to gain the highest marks. For many years, CSE and GCSE examiners have known that some pupils find this a difficult task and have produced 'triple deckers' (questions in three parts), or similarly graded questions demanding longer and more complex answers to each successive part.

As long ago as 1968, Moffett commented on the tendency of many children to condense their ideas when committing them to paper, and to leave many points implicit rather than making them explicit. He suggested that the ability to generalize and to write more explicitly usually improved with age:

> Whether they are writing stories or ideas, children over-condense at first and only later become able to elaborate and expand. But many underdeveloped high school students have the same limitations; they write only synopses and one can feel their reluctance to leave the haven of narrative.

Moffett went on to suggest that factors such as the social class of the pupils might be important in explaining differing writing abilities, and this is an hypothesis which we explore elsewhere in this book. For the moment though, it is more important to emphasize the extent and complexity of the hidden rules and expectations that teachers and examiners have, so that readers can be alerted to the need to think more critically about the formulation of assessment tasks in their own teaching, and consider what help to give those pupils who habitually fail to give enough detail in their answers. (We also refer the reader back to the related issue of '*selective* explicitness' in Chapter 2.) Bearing this in mind, we therefore turn to an examination of more sustained writing tasks.

Accounts and essays

Our school survey revealed that the words 'account' and 'essay' were used indiscriminately by teachers to refer to a piece of continuous writing that might have an average length of from one to three pages (approximately 200–600 words). In geography, such writing was predominantly descriptive and explanatory; in history there were also deductive exercises to test pupils' command of the use of evidence and more imaginative pieces of writing. In RE and social studies, the account was often an exercise designed to encourage pupils to explore and assess their own moral attitude towards an issue. Since the advent of GCSE, there has been a noticeable decline in the use of the essay form as a means of assessment, compared with GCE, though children still have to master the art of writing sustained prose for much project and coursework, and extended pieces of writing still have a place in final examinations as well.

In our survey, some lessons were very formal, and here pupils were often asked to write accounts or essays about the topic covered in the lesson. As well as having to write sustained prose, they also had to follow a logical structure in their explanation. Some of the pupils seemed to face difficulties because they did not know what questions to mentally ask themselves as part of the structuring process and once again this helps us to explain the tendency to over-condense. If the teacher provided a list of guide questions on the board, they were happier, but if this was not the case, then they lacked the humanities equivalent of the scientific report format to help them structure their writing. The well-worn 'introduction, main points, conclusion' formula briefly offered by some teachers was too vague to be of any real use. The pupils most sensitive to the rules for getting by in this kind of situation cued in to the teacher's change of tone as he or she began to talk about a topic, or to summarize some information. As soon as they were aware that some writing might be involved, certain pupils would take out their jotters and begin to make notes as the teacher spoke, whereas others just sat and listened. When the piece of writing was set, the teacher's exposition of the topic had usually provided the necessary logical structure for it. The pupils who had made notes therefore had a head start in writing their account. This was particularly valuable given the brevity of some titles – e.g. 'Describe the buildings (type and arrangement) of the centre of any large city you know'. There may be a number of reasons why pupils don't take notes in such circumstances. Some will be trusting to their memories, but others may fail to read the teacher's cues about the task, while yet others will take a deliberate decision to avoid the extra work involved in two lots of writing instead of one. Writing was defined as 'hard work' by most pupils, to be avoided if possible, especially if they lacked interest in the lesson.

Even when the lessons were not traditional in character, this attitude persisted. It was well-illustrated by pupils engaged in a local history project. Small groups concentrated on finding out about different aspects of the development of a local town: transport, education, housing, etc. They visited the town, took photographs, interviewed people and used the archives of the local library. The resulting information was to be used to write brief chapters of a joint topic that would have a 'real' purpose as it would be on display in the school library and available for other pupils to use. The pupils engaged in the detective work enthusiastically, finding and analysing a good range of primary and secondary evidence. The finished project was, however, disappointing. Most chapters had an introduction of sorts, but then collapsed into a miscellaneous 'scrapbook' of information that lacked order and coherence, similar to the canals example described above in the section on notes. It would be easy to dismiss this failure as being due to their perception of the writing as 'hard work', and it is certainly true that the excitement of the search and the opportunity of working outside school are stronger motivators than the thought of having your work on display. But for a number of reasons, this task may be beyond the skill level of the average 13- to 14-year-old. Here are pupils relatively unpractised in operating rules for structuring accounts themselves. In many lessons, their teachers will have been using the techniques we have described above, which do not actively engage pupils in learning ways of organizing their work. Add to this the fact that they will not be particularly familiar with the kind of local history pamphlets that somehow manage to create a coherent story of development out of snippets of information. Neither do they have the depth of knowledge that can provide an overview of a topic and help to make sense of the fragments of local evidence that are available. This is not to argue that the children have somehow not yet matured to the right intellectual stage to cope, because that would imply some sort of biological determinant of intellectual development that it is difficult to prove. Rather, what we can say for certain is that they have not been given the necessary tools to do the job. Here we have considered both cognitive and communicative ground rules, which are essential for the completion of the task. These need to be explored by teachers in connection with all tasks, but unfortunately can often only be easily recognized after the exercise has been set, when the failure of some pupils can highlight them.

Another very mechanical kind of account-writing limited children's ability to learn the constructional rules for themselves by having to engage actively with the material. It involved writing summaries or 'translations' of information contained in textbooks. Here, structuring work was not really a problem; the important task

was to display to the teacher that you had learned something from the exercise
and were not just copying blindly from the book. Again, some of the apparently
less-involved pupils showed a marked preference for copying, because it
involved less effort and no engagement with the work, leaving the mind free to
roam (such pupils often enjoy copying diagrams for the same reason). 'Can't we
just copy it out?' was a phrase often heard from some corner of the room when
these tasks were set. Pupils commented on the skill required to put the
complicated prose of the textbook into their own words, to prove they
understood it. This was not a task that they particularly enjoyed and they made
comparisons between this kind of routine work and the greater opportunity to
write about their personal opinions which RE and social studies provided:

> You've got more scope because you aren't being spoon-fed education. You're
> asked to think about it. And you don't necessarily have a right or wrong answer,
> it's just your opinion.

Obviously, this was a great motivator and some vindication of the view that
children need to use personal and expressive language as part of their learning.
But the sceptic might also observe that some children saw this kind of writing as
easier because it was an opportunity for them to reiterate everyday knowledge
and opinions rather than wrestle with new information within the framework of
a discipline. We know that that is not necessarily the case, however, because
expressive writing can have a sound underpinning of subject knowledge, social
and economic geography in this case:

Lake Maracaibo

In the past: a group of dirty mud huts on the edge of a stinking slimy lake. In the
present: a South American Geneva or a booming Manchester. What happened to
the lake dwellers? Gurgling oil pipelines under their huts. Telegraph wires
overhead. Their stilted primitive homes being destroyed by oil and spluttering
tankers.

The new lake dweller: Mr Smith with a job (good prospects, travel passes, three
weeks holiday a year) at the oil refinery. Mrs Smith belonging to the Women's
Institute; Friday, shop at the supermarket, Monday bridge, and Wednesday, visit
Mother. Smith junior, attending a state school perhaps, and if there is one, going
to Sunday school.

The architects, a dreamland, space as much as desired. New, clean, pros-
perous.

The builders' paradise, houses to be built.

Who makes a profit? The owner of the oil company, the ship-owner, the
builders, the shop-keepers.

What would happen if some egg-head in the future invents something easier
than oil, cheaper than oil? Would the Smiths build a house on stilts? Would Mr
Smith fish in the muddy waters? Would Mrs Smith grow potatoes in the mud?
Who would make a loss? The oil company owners, the ship-owners, the builders,

the shop-keepers? Would the Smiths go north to rich North America? South to Brazil? (Boy aged 13 years)

The important thing is to be aware of what sense the children are making of the lesson. Many humanities teachers, like their colleagues in science teaching, shy away from accepting the use of more personal or expressive language, because, as with imaginative exercises, they fear the loss of 'disciplined' thinking. But often, as in the note-taking we discussed earlier, it is personal language and so-called 'expressive writing' which can increase children's involvement and also help us to gauge their level of understanding, as in the example above and the one which follows. Here, after a geography lesson, the pupils were simply asked to describe what they had done. Here is one pupil's brief and perceptive response:

> In the lesson we discussed Africa and Britain saying words which were thought of when thinking of the two different countries. If you notice most words connected with Africa are bad and words connected with Britain are good.

Here we have a pupil confidently talking directly to the teacher, with a clear grasp of both the purpose of the lesson and the rules of the task. However, there can still be pupils with difficulties. The following is a much more lengthy and detailed account where there is no evidence that the pupil understood the purpose of what was happening:

> In our last Geography lesson we drew two columns and labelled each one, one Britain and the other Africa. Then we wrote under each one words we thought described the countryside in Africa and in Britain. Then in the middle of one page we wrote Africa and in the middle of another page we put Britain. Then Mr. A. went round the class asking for one word of their list to put down on my copy, and we did the same for Britain. Mr. A. then handed out some photographs and we got into groups and had to sort out the cards into three groups, one photograph which described Africa, another which described Britain, and the last pile ones we didn't know.

The writing is reminiscent of the boy in Chapter 2 who didn't understand at all what the purpose of his experiment was in a biology lesson and just gave a description of what he did. However, unless we interview the pupil involved here, we don't know for certain that she has missed the purpose of the lesson, only that she has interpreted the task as a *description* of what happened in the lesson, rather than an *explanation* of what she learned from it. It is the children's decision to use one set of rules to complete the task by, rather than another, which leads to the inadequate or adequate performance.

Some teachers fear that more personal forms of writing will prevent children from developing understanding informed by the particular perspectives of subject disciplines. By keeping to formal language they hope to concentrate pupils' minds on the cognitive rules that underpin the discipline in question and this, of course, restricts their choice of writing task. As in science, humanities teachers in our survey were divided into different camps over the use of specialist terminology and impersonal language. In geography, pupils were rewarded for using the appropriate terminology, but different teachers emphasized different reasons for doing so. One teacher explained:

> I expect pupils to use geographical terms where appropriate, e.g. the factors influencing the pattern of communication are relief and drainage, rather than: roads and railways go where they go because some bits of highland and rivers and bogs make things difficult in places.

This teacher preferred his pupils to use the specialist terms because he saw them as more 'economical' and also because they were required by examiners. He added that he did not give formal definitions, but talked about the term and similar words for it with the class. His pupils were then expected to pick up the use of these words and incorporate them in their written accounts. Other geography teachers also emphasized the constraints that examinations imposed, but, like the science teachers referred to in Chapter 2, felt that subjective language and 'flowery' prose distracted pupils from the task of understanding the geographical aspects of what was being studied.

Such apprehensions also lead many teachers to reject the use of imaginative tasks in geography, and they may well feel that some weight is lent to their argument by the example quoted by Michael Williams (1981). The exercise set by the teacher asked the pupil to 'Imagine you are a traveller crossing the West from St Louis to the Pacific'. This is the response of a 14-year-old girl:

> As the oxen walked along the wagon wheels slowly turned, we heard a cry, and indian cry. as I lifted my head I saw a crowd of Indians on the hill. We called the oxen to 'stop' said dad. 'Dad dad quick' i said 'look, they have got guns, quick get ours' Dad got the guns but did not draw them ready to shoot because he did not know what they wanted. The indians got their horses and walked to Dad and said 'get movin we don't want to see you on our vally again, get movin'. (Williams, 1981, p. 49)

Most geography teachers would be unhappy with this piece of writing, not mainly because of the inadequacies of punctuation and grammar, but because it does not convey much geographical knowledge. As Williams comments:

> The writer, who intended to describe a desperate, thrilling encounter may not have appreciated fully what the teacher's intentions were. Certainly, rivers, mountains and plateaux of The West do not feature prominently in her narrative, though we can infer that this was a major objective of the original task.

As with the imaginative tasks we analysed in Chapter 2, the problem is that the teacher has failed to communicate the particular ground rules for this piece of work. It is meant to be an interesting vehicle for the display of knowledge about the physical features of the American West. The teacher understands the value of providing a variety of written tasks, but when the pupil is confronted with an exercise beginning 'Imagine you are . . .', she automatically begins to apply the set of rules she would use in an English lesson 'adventure story' exercise. No doubt with sufficient preliminary work on the part of the teacher, pupils like this would be capable of producing more satisfactory pieces of work; it is a case of devising strategies to draw more attention to the rules that frame the task. Without careful teaching, therefore, personal writing and imaginative tasks may carry dangers. But if the teacher is aware of the reasons for the problems, such writing tasks can successfully be incorporated into the repertoire. In fact, if children can successfully perform the wider range of writing tasks, then we have a much better assessment of their real level of understanding.

Our sensitivity to the ground rules that pupils are using can help to explain many of the problems of understanding that arise in the classroom. An exercise from the Schools Council History Project demonstrates this most forcefully, and shows us the underlying logic in what seem at first to be most illogical statements from pupils. Thirteen-year-olds were using a 'Detective Work' simulation exercise in order to better understand some of the problems of interpreting evidence. The task was to solve the case of a mysterious death by using a set of clues – items taken from a dead man's wallet – and logically deduce the most likely cause of death: it is probably a hit-and-run accident, but there is no definite proof. There were a number of seemingly illogical answers from the children, with complicated plotting based on speculation only flimsily supported by the evidence, if at all. Inventive stories were woven around the characters who appeared in the clues:

> . . . as he was walking with the money he was attacked by the girl and her mates [the girl on picture in wallet] . . . it was the girl on the picture who got him because she was envious about him going to Katt's party.

> This is a wild guess, but I think Jeff killed Mark. I also think that Mark must have had some enemies if Jeff didn' kill him.

At first glance, we tend to reject these as immature and illogical thinking styles. However, the pupils *are* using a coherent form of deductive reasoning, but they end up with the wrong answer because their interpretive framework of ground rules is not the one the teacher expects them to use for formal reasoning tasks in school. Both of the answers above begin to make sense if we see the problem from the children's point of view. Through conversations with them, they revealed that either seriously or for fun, they were coping with the problem by using the model of the television 'thriller'. They had worked out their own set of rules for how to find the culprit in thrillers. To make the plot exciting, any death is usually a murder rather than an accident; the culprit nearly always appears in the scenario but is unlikely to be suspected; and there is always a satisfactory conclusion – a definite 'right answer' where the villain is exposed. The children's answers conform beautifully to the kind of logical system which they had worked out for themselves but, of course, it is not the one employed by teachers and by successful pupils. Those who have come to the task with a framework that is inappropriate for school do not have markedly inferior cognitive processes but, for one reason or another, they are insensitive to the interpretive framework for this task. All their previous 'everyday' experience of mysterious deaths has come to them from the television, and therefore they have simply used the same sort of deductive rules in the classroom, not realizing that the deductive processes of real-life detectives are shaped by different factors. They have been very good at working out the tricks of television drama, and so they are sophisticated thinkers in some ways but not in others.

Understanding this kind of difficulty can also help us to analyse more clearly the nature of the cognitive problems that pupils face in two other areas: becoming critical observers in social science, and completing tasks designed to encourage 'empathetic' responses in history.

Peter Medway (1980), an English specialist and humanities teacher, cites a project that two girls completed for him. It was an account about the Mecca Dance Hall, which they frequently visited. He was expecting the pupils, with his guidance, to produce some basic anthropological and sociological insights, based on their experiences there. In the event, they wrote a diary of their evening at the Mecca, which took the social context completely for granted, rather than making it the object of their observations. While Medway wanted some kind of ethnography, the girls produced writing governed by the set of rules they considered to be appropriate for the task as they perceived it, i.e. writing about the fun they had. A strong advocate of interdisciplinary, self-directed project work, based on expressive writing, Medway accounted for their failure by invoking the concept of cognitive immaturity. He doubted that children of secondary school age are capable of, or interested in, engaging in formal 'disciplined' thinking. But this seems to be an unduly pessimistic conclusion. Though he may well be right in suggesting that children of secondary age particularly enjoy what he calls 'celebratory' writing – writing that gives status and value to their everyday experiences – there is no reason to suppose that they are incapable of thinking and writing in other ways. But the teaching strategy would have to change, because it is unlikely that 'disciplined thinking' would emerge without more guidance of some sort, as essentially it means thinking framed by the specialist teacher's cognitive ground rules. In this particular case, the teacher might perhaps concentrate on ideas such as what sense a 'stranger' from another society or planet would make of what was going on at the Mecca, or do some comparative work on the rituals of everyday life. When teachers and writers like Williams (1977) argue that expressive writing traps children in their common-sense knowledge, it is this kind of problem that is being addressed. Fortunately, by considering the role of ground rules, we can see that it is not the language *per se* which traps the children's thought, and that, with the use of appropriate teaching techniques, children can engage in 'disciplined' thought when using any of a wide range of writing styles.

The empathy question

Bearing the above conclusions in mind, let us now turn to the vexed question of exercises in empathy. Vexed, because since their institution in various GCSE history examinations, they have been the subject of much misunderstanding and controversy. Traditionalists have sniped at the 'flights of fancy' that empathy exercises sometimes result ·in, while more 'progressive' teachers have emphasized the increased understanding and enjoyment that can emerge from such tasks. In a book of this nature there is no place for a detailed examination of the complex arguments surrounding the debate, but it is possible to highlight one area. Those who believe that empathy is an aspect of understanding that has a valuable place in the study of history usually differentiate between 'everyday' empathy and genuine historical empathy. We shall therefore look at the main thrusts of their argument in this respect.

We need to begin by understanding what empathy means in various contexts. In the everyday world, of course, having empathy with someone's situation means that we can see things from their point of view rather than our own. Teachers of many humanities subjects may find it useful to encourage pupils to empathize with the situation of others in order to arrive at a clearer understanding of the reasons for their actions. In social studies, for instance, role-play exercises encourage white pupils to empathize with someone who is a victim of racial prejudice and discrimination, to understand the sort of responses they may have. The success of such exercises depends on pupils answering the question: 'How would you feel if this happened to you?' In one famous exercise, for example, certain pupils wear distinguishing arm bands, and gradually become the victims of abuse by others. In other exercises, there is an attempt to provide information that will allow pupils to project themselves into the real-life situation of others. For example, Action Aid's teaching pack on Third World images provides excellent material on reasons why many married couples in Third World countries choose to have large families. Using such material it becomes easier for children to understand why many poor families do not practise birth control. This too involves an empathetic response: children have to learn to discard their own ethnocentric attitudes and judgements and take on the perceptions and arguments of others. Sometimes material can be presented to pupils that is based on actual case studies, and in these cases pupils are able to empathize with particular others who really exist. But even if the empathy is with groups – victims of prejudice and many Third World families – rather than specific people, this does not detract from its value as an aid to knowledge and understanding. Another characteristic of empathy is that it does not exist in a vacuum. Empathizing is a skill that is dependent upon either a body of knowledge (in the case of the Third World family), or on involvement in experiences that mimic the situation of the person with whom the pupil is attempting to empathize (the role-play example).

No-one has doubted the usefulness and validity of the kind of exercises described above, but heated debates have surrounded the use of empathy in written history tasks, so we will concentrate on this in detail, as it can illustrate particularly well how useful it is to identify hidden ground rules associated with both cognitive and communicative aspects of this kind of exercise.

Perhaps one of the difficulties may lie in the relative remoteness of the historical periods being studied. We can readily see that it might be easier to empathize with a victim of prejudice in one's own society, and that it is more difficult to empathize with a distant family in a Third World country with different customs, norms and values. Consequently, to empathize with people in a society remote in terms of both time and place, is obviously likely to be a challenge. But it is not this gradation of difficulty that most writers concentrate on. Instead, they choose to discern a break or distinction between everyday and historical empathy, and it is this distinction that is the subject of the following analysis.

Among others, the Southern Regional Examinations Board decided to include empathy as one of the historical skills to be tested by the GCSE. In its explanatory leaflet (SREB, 1986), the Board accepts that historical empathy is dependent upon a foundation of factual information. It then goes on to suggest that there are three levels of empathetic response, and the marks awarded should reflect:

1 Everyday empathy
   (twentieth century motives, feelings and attitudes applied to the past).
2 Stereotyped historical empathy
   (there is one point of view characteristic of a particular time).
3 Differentiated historical empathy
   (different groups and individuals in the past had different points of view).

Such a description would suggest that at the most satisfactory level of historical empathy (level 3), the principal skill required is the ability to shake off twentieth-century rules of thought and, knowing sufficient about particular historical characters or groups and their time, attempt to understand the meanings they give to circumstances and events, their attitudes and motivation, their actions and reactions (as far as it is possible to do so).

Controversy has partly centred around exercises that encourage pupils to imaginatively project themselves into certain historical situations and 'take it from there'. Here is what Booth *et al.* (1987, p. 25), for example, have to say at the start of their discussion of such empathy exercises:

History teachers have for a long time sought ways to elicit good empathetic responses from their pupils. Often this has been in the form of the instruction 'Imagine you are . . .'. Sensitively handled, with adequate preparation, this kind of exercise may still work. However, many of us have been disappointed by the results, probably for two reasons. First, there is no real guidance in such an instruction as to whether to write a work of complete fiction or simply recall the facts of the story.

Nor is a completely factual piece with an imaginative gloss quite what we are looking for.

The authors are suggesting that, provided the ground rules are properly laid down, the information may be historically valid, rather than simply being wild imaginings. However, it is likely to be factual information rather than genuine empathetic understanding. Thus it may have a part to play in learning, but it is no test of empathy. It has much more in common with the American West example discussed earlier. Our own survey of such tasks in history lessons revealed the importance of clearly communicating the various rules of this particular writing game. In one lesson, the pupils were asked to write a speech where Richard III defends himself against a charge of murdering his two nephews. First, it was not made clear to the pupils whether Richard was being tried in his own lifetime or in the 'courtroom of history'. Consequently, some of the pupils omitted evidence that was provided by writers living after the time of Richard's death. (In fact, of course, he was never on trial – a complication of the exercise that could only serve to confuse the pupils further, yet this was a suggested task in a modern and very popular textbook.) More importantly, however, some pupils saw this as an imaginative task similar to one they might be given in an English lesson. For them it was a chance to write a 'ripping yarn' – concocting fantastic alibis for Richard in the process. Others, who of course gained the highest marks, saw it as an academic task, where it was essential to incorporate as much as they possibly could of the factual information they had learned in the previous lessons.

In interviews, some pupils were pretty confident that they had mastered the particular set of rules for this kind of exercise. In this extract, for instance, four girls were being questioned. Enthusiastic group comments (in brackets) intersperse one pupil's explanation:

> When it says pretend say, you're a Norman knight attacking a castle [yes]. Well, it's told you what actually happened when the knights attacked the castle [yes] so you've got to write down being a Norman knight [yes, yes]. What you felt like, plus you've got to add what actually did happen [oh, yes, yes].

Some of the pupils could also clearly see that different ground rules operated in English and history lessons:

> In History an essay I've written has been about if I was a knight fighting against another army, but these essays don't seem like essays done in English. They seem to be more on the information side.

In another lesson pupils were asked to imagine they were evacuees, and write a letter home to their parents. There was extensive class discussion about the type of information that could be included in the letter, and many pupils performed the task to the teacher's satisfaction, displaying an array of information about the

Home Front in the course of their writing. The following is a short extract from one pupil's work:

> Have you had many Air-raids in Birmingham? We've had a few practices. We go underneath the school in the corridors. It is dark, dusty and hot because of the boiler. Amy has to go in some holes in the ground for the air-raid practices which the male teachers dug before they went off to war.
> Mrs. Rice's husband has gone so she has some land girls from London to help on the farm. I think Mrs. Rice is very kind because she took us in when she had the four land girls from London to feed and bed. I like one of them called Jenny. She is nice and speaks funny.
> Everybody at school laughs when I talk so I try to laugh with them, but it's very hard. Cath likes how I speak so she defends me a bit. Amy hasn't got anybody to stand up for her so she keeps asking to go home and she cries at night. Will you come and see us? I know you have your job at the bomb factory, but can't they spare you for a day so you can come and see us?

This is obviously a *tour de force* of imaginative writing by a 13-year-old girl who fully understands the importance of weaving in and displaying her historical knowledge. In contrast, another girl writes the sort of letter she might write to her mum today. She focuses mainly on the things that are close to her heart: kindness, food, animals. In that sense, it is realistic, indeed perhaps much more true to life than the first example, but it is less successful because it could be describing any holiday in the country, and is not such a clear display of knowledge about wartime Britain. The pupil leaves implicit the reasons for her move to the country and there are no definite clues that this is in fact wartime. In addition, there are problems of anachronistic expressions, etc.:

> Dear Mum and Dad,
>
> Missing you very much. and I hope you are well. Realy enjoying myself and Mr and Mrs Cuttle are realy nice and kind to me. I have got my own bed room and it has got a bason under the bed and that was for if I needed the toilet eregently. I am on a farm in the country and it is grate. Yesterday I started my new school and have made four new freinds. We have done Maths, English and some Drawing. it is the weekend now and I am helping in the yard. So far I have milked some cows and some goats. which was fun. Mr and Mrs Cuttle have gots Four old English Sheep dogs and one ginger tom cat. I am not very keen on the food. that Mrs Cuttle make but I like her bread. They bouth grow vegetibels and those are very nice. Missing you very much hope to see you soon.

But there are more fundamental problems about the nature of this task. Are these pieces of writing in fact examples of pupils engaging in 'historical empathy'? It seems doubtful, because what they are employing is what most writers characterize as 'everyday empathy' – modern motives, feelings and attitudes applied to the past. For, if the teacher provides plenty of information about the process of evacuation and leaves it to the children to imagine 'what it must have felt like', then the children are likely to engage in two processes in order to cope with the task. The first will be what Shemilt (1984) calls 'imaginative reconstruction' – they will create in their own minds the sights and sounds of the railway station thronged with labelled children, or the new home in the countryside. Along with this they may expect that evacuees experienced various emotions, similar to those suffered by the pupils themselves in similar situations: stomach-churning fear and apprehension, homesickness, excitement or a feeling of strangeness. So what such an exercise can offer is the chance to do a lively piece of writing, display some factual knowledge and experience a feeling of 'common humanity' with those in the past. For many children, and adults too for that matter, part of the fun of learning history is the pleasure gained from imaginatively projecting oneself into the past and 'acting out' what it must have been like (for example, television's 'The Good Old Days', Victorian Fun Days and the Sealed Knot Society of Civil War enthusiasts). Such exercises as the one above capitalize on that imaginative yearning, as well as attempting to test children's knowledge. But we must recognize such tasks for what they are and not make the assumption that personal imaginative projection and historical empathy are necessarily the same thing. In the examples above, the first girl has read the cues correctly, and produced an excellent piece of work, but the limited scope of the task means that she can only display a low level of response in terms of genuine historical empathy.

Shemilt (1984, p. 67) scathingly parodies the principal forms of writing that are associated with 'everyday empathy' exercises:

> . . . this takes one of three forms: the direct invocation to project one's psyche into the past ('Imagine you are a rat on the North-West Passage . . .', and so on); the personal diary ('You are a Toltec warrior about to be sacrificed to Huitzilopochtli: complete your diary for the day'); and the letter home, most usually from one illiterate to another.

So if such exercises tend to be badly done, it is largely the teacher's problem, because, even if the pupils interpret the ground rules satisfactorily, they can hardly do more than write good 'historical fiction'. A further criticism is that for years teachers and examiners have interpreted empathy skills as being largely to do with the affective domain, where pupils concentrate on exploring the emotions and feelings of their subjects (perhaps due both to confusion between the concepts of empathy and sympathy, and of imagination and emotion; or the desire for an alternative romantic experience of history). There is now a common consensus among examiners that empathy involves taking on the interpretations of events that people in the past would themselves hold. If empathy is about the ability to step into the minds of people in the past, then it is about pupils' cognitive behaviour as well as affective empathy:

> Empathetic construction should be taught and assessed as a cognitive not an affective activity more akin to the elaboration and justification of hypotheses than to creative writing. (Shemilt, 1984, p. 79)

It is also likely that such an approach would significantly reduce the amount of misinterpretation of the ground rules that results in pupils writing 'historical fiction', as they would be far less likely to confuse the ground rules operating in history lessons with those required in many of their tasks in English.

So how do pupils learn 'real' historical empathy skills? And what sort of tasks will produce writing with empathetic characteristics? First, most writers take a developmental view that sees the adolescent mind maturing from the stage of 'everyday empathy' to the stage of genuine historical empathy, displaying an ability to shed twentieth-century perceptions and recreate an 'alien world view' (Shemilt, 1984). SREB (1986) would add that pupils have to be aware that there is not one stereotyped alien world view, but that different individuals or groups in a particular historical period would have different views. This is considered to be the highest level of development of empathy. Such a developmental view suggests that the ability will only come with time, and therefore places limits on what the teacher can actively do to help.

Secondly, most authorities also now urge that empathy questions should be very tightly structured, to encourage pupils towards empathetic *explanations*, which can be drawn from a limited supply of stimulus material or previous background knowledge. One of the most trenchant criticisms of empathy exercises must be that children are bound to fall back on everyday modes of thinking when confronted with a task about which they have insufficient information, and in the light of our analysis this advice is obviously sound. So, instead of the broad canvas provided by the 'Imagine you are' questions, teachers need to provide evidence about real people's attitudes and behaviour, which then require some sort of explanation. This should help to orient the child towards cognitive activity rather than everyday affective empathy. Booth *et al.* (1987) give a good example of such a question. In connection with work on the First World War, pupils might be asked: 'If it was so awful in the trenches, why did people choose to join up and stay there?' This is also a particularly useful example of a task that helps us to discriminate between the 'imaginative reconstruction' involved in summoning up the objective conditions of trench warfare, and the empathetic understanding that can explain why soldiers stuck it, a task which involves understanding ideas and attitudes ranging from the prevailing jingoistic nationalism, through a rational fear of the death sentence for desertion, to the psychological pressure of the white feather – a combination of both universal human responses and those conditioned by the prevailing attitudes of a particular age. Such dissection of a question gives us a much clearer understanding of the qualities we are looking for in a written answer.

Such tasks transform the empathy enterprise into more rigorous historical analysis and understanding, and away from the murky waters of fiction and flights of fancy in an historical setting. However, we are still left in a difficult situation as assessors of pupils' work. Currently, examination boards argue that everyday empathy is worthy of reward, as it marks the earliest stage in the adolescent's development of more authentic historical empathy. But within everyday empathy some writers distinguish between ideas and attitudes conditioned by the circumstances of life in the twentieth century, and other emotions or ways of thinking that are common throughout time (although this too is a controversial area). So it could be equally valid to argue that at their earlier stage of development, pupils should only be rewarded for expressing universal emotions and attitudes, because to impose distinctively twentieth-century feelings and motives on historical actors is patently wrong and should not therefore be rewarded. But if we accept the developmental view, there is no way that immature minds can distinguish between the particular and the universal. So the immature writer pours forth his collection of everyday empathetic thoughts and feelings. They are rewarded. If by chance they are universal rather than particular, he can be further rewarded, though he himself does not have the capacity to discriminate between the two. It is hardly any wonder at all that controversy rages around this issue, when, under our present examination system, pupils might be rewarded for arbitrary leaps from everyday to historical empathy and for not being able to distinguish the universal from the particular.

However, there is another way of looking at the problem. Like Medway's view of children's thinking in social science, which we discussed earlier in this chapter, many history teachers' views on empathy are linked to an explicit or implicit developmental psychology. This leads them to suggest that pre-empathetic responses or everyday empathy deserve credit because they are the inevitable precursors of genuine historical empathy, and characteristic of a certain stage of development which it is therefore valid to test in a history examination. On the other hand, not all cognitive psychologists are so determinedly developmental. For example, Donaldson's (1978) work has much in common with the concepts of ground rules and frames that we have employed so far in this book. In criticizing Piaget's view that young children are cognitively egocentric, Donaldson argues that, provided children have the ground rules of a task clearly explained to them, they can see cognitive problems from another person's point of view. Such findings cast doubt on the accepted view that teachers must wait until children's 'natural' development allows them to arrive at a different stage of thinking. Instead, it throws the responsibility on to the teacher to clearly reveal the rules that circumscribe the task. If pupils are at the stage where they are using 'everyday empathy' it is because, for one reason or another, they are using taken-for-granted, commonsense frameworks for interpreting the demands of the task. But the cause would appear to be social, rather than some inevitable inbuilt immaturity. Perhaps they have not really been given the opportunity to learn the alternative interpretations that, paradoxically, are taken-for-granted by specialist history teachers as the way in which one properly empathizes with historical actors. This is particularly so when pupils are confronted with a selection of stimulus material to make sense of for themselves. They are obviously likely to respond using their commonly held 'everyday' sets of cognitive and affective ground rules. Other pupils may not choose to bother making the effort, particularly because good empathetic understanding must be based on extensive historical knowledge. Even those who do try may be frustrated by their own lack of knowledge. If we look at the kind of errors being made by children in the empathy exercises we have discussed above, we can clearly see how the teachers' shortcomings, as well as the pupils', have led to inadequate performance of the task. Somewhere along the line the teacher must ensure that the rules get revealed in the most effective way, as for example in 'disconfirmation' exercises. Here pupils are given some information about an event and then asked to predict its outcome. Often there is a mismatch between their predictions and the real historical outcome. A follow-up discussion will reveal the basis on which the pupils made their predictions, which can then be compared with the attitudes, values and motives of the historical characters involved.

But such framework theory must therefore also lead us to modify the developmentalists' approach. Though writers may choose to construct a model that groups children's written answers into increasingly competent levels of response, we have no evidence to suggest that individual children progress steadily through each stage. Rather, children's cognitive response to any problem they are set is to choose any particular set of ground rules that they think is appropriate for the task in hand. Impetuous responses, of course, are especially likely to involve the use of 'everyday' rules and thus 'everyday empathy', as are responses where the teacher provides little guidance. Left entirely to their own devices, groups of children may do little more than pool their own ignorance; though the teacher's guidance can be subtle and indirect, it must none the less be there. Given the opportunity to use alternative frameworks, they can reject everyday ones as inadequate for genuine historical empathy. That comes as a result of their reflexive thinking – their ability to consider for themselves their choice of ground rules – and may only occur after discussion with others and their teacher. Thus one child, quoted by Shemilt (1984, p. 73), reflects on his failure to explain the behaviour of a Puritan Pamphleteer after being brutally punished by Elizabeth I:

> I got it wrong because I thought how I'd react if the queen did that to me. I forgot that I'm not a Puritan and don't live in the sixteenth century.

The key skill, then, is the ability to think reflexively, and realizing this fact helps us to demystify the concept of empathy.

If we do modify the developmentalist argument in this way, it also forces us to ask the question, is it justifiable to reward pupils for what they are not doing? In other words, do we have to reject the idea that pupils should be rewarded for expressing twentieth-century everyday empathy? If pupils have not yet made that leap of understanding into the minds of others (and we are well aware of the limits to authenticity in such an endeavour), or even realized that that is the task which is required of them, they are not engaged in the kind of reflexive thinking that is the basis of disciplined historical analysis and understanding. That certainly sounds a pessimistic note. On the other hand, we can more optimistically say that sensitive teaching strategies may provide the answer by exposing and exploring the ground rules that underlie empathy questions. That will allow us to see historical empathy as a more readily attainable skill, if it is indeed one we consider to be of value.

4 Ground rules in English lessons

Writing in English lessons

Learning in English is almost entirely a matter of acquiring cultural competences of one kind or another. Even the layout of a letter is a socially prescribed convention that some children learn at home before meeting it at school. A folk tale too – to take a contrasting example – also exemplifies a set of cultural competences, which some children become familiar with early in life through bedtime stories. In this case, the competences include not merely such a formula as 'Once upon a time', but more profound aspects of the story such as the persons, situations and events that characterize the genre. We could continue through such forms as the English essay, the critical commentary on a work of literature, and the formal 'business letter': learning to manage these is partly a matter of learning cultural expectations, and what can be done within each of them. Because the 'cultural expectations' in question include not just layout and conventional phrases such as 'Yours faithfully', but more intangible conventions about content and style, it can be said that the subject English is centrally concerned with the teaching and learning of ground rules.

Although it is sometimes said that school English has no content for pupils to learn, this is far from the truth. Not only does English teach ground rules, but among these ground rules are prescriptions for content in a more literal sense. Because speech and writing must be about something, any work that pupils do in English must have a content, and in some circumstances this takes on great importance. It is well known that in the assessment of essays in English examinations such as GCSE English Language, the elements that carry the greatest weight are the content and its arrangement in the text. Indeed, it is perfectly proper for this to be so, as we would not wish to equate 'good writing' solely with an acceptable style and mastery of the conventions of spelling and punctuation. It is essential that the content of writing is given prominence not only in assessment but in the purposes and priorities of the pupils. Good writing is writing that says something well: the 'something' that is being expressed cannot be excluded from this conception of 'good writing', for it is impossible to conceive of good writing that says nothing whatsoever of any importance. The direction taken by English teaching during the last two decades has reinforced this. During the 1960s, it became commonplace for English teachers that pupils wrote best when they wrote about something that mattered to them and did so for some reader who was interested to read what they had to say, though this was often themselves or a sympathetic teacher. This placed an overt emphasis on the choice of content and its importance for the writers.

This emphasis brought with it some important implications. As English was intended to focus upon the ability to read and write (and, more recently, to talk), it was necessary to find topics that were apparently accessible to all pupils. At the same time, most English teachers in secondary schools were being trained in university schools of English literature, so that for them it was literary models of writing that were most important for their pupils to emulate. These two influences converged during the late 1960s and early 1970s to produce sets of ground rules that remain very powerful, even though their existence is not always clearly recognized by the English teachers themselves.

Because many pupils wrote best about topics that were of direct interest to them in their present lives, rather than about topics chosen by adults, it became usual for English teachers to look for topics within their pupils' everyday experience. But not any topic would be acceptable; nor would every way of writing about them. The models were literary, especially certain genres of quasi-realistic fiction, including the prose and verse of D. H. Lawrence.

> The world is of interest, in this treatment, purely as it affects the experiencing self, and hardly at all as a reality which has an existence independently of the student, one which was there before and will continue after the student's participation in it. (Medway, 1986b)

Such writing belongs to the Romantic tradition with its celebration of individual sensitivity and the expression of heightened states of mind. Although in the 'personal' mode much importance is given to the appearance of authenticity in the representation of the writer's experience, successful writing in this mode is never simple and unmediated, for it depends as much as any other kind of language upon the ground rules of the genre from which it is drawn. Some English teachers may believe that they are encouraging their pupils to look into their hearts; what they are in fact doing is helping them to operate in certain literary modes that have become so familiar to the teachers as to be invisible.

Indeed, what older pupils write often proves to be more consciously managed than seems to be implied in the teachers' rhetoric of authentic first-hand experience. Writing of this kind is skilful rather than passionate: the writer looks for effects rather than seeking to reveal his or her soul. At best, such writing is witty, inventive and entertaining, and reaches towards highbrow journalism or *belles lettres*, and the capacity to write in a lively and inventive way about any topic. Clearly, this is an important and valuable ability, though only a minority of more able pupils achieve it at school. With less able pupils, however, the desire to show off their language resources often becomes obtrusive, and leads to clumsy displays of 'fine writing'.

The foregoing paragraphs summarize some of the results of a study of English teaching in schools and colleges called *Versions of English* (Barnes *et al.*, 1984). In the remainder of this chapter we shall often refer to this material, which is based on lessons taught to 15- to 18-year-olds; but we shall also make use of a study of English lessons taught to 12-year-old pupils that was carried out by Peter Medway (1986a). This latter study showed that the kinds of writing set to 12-year-olds in middle and secondary schools, though different in certain respects from the writing done by older students, is nevertheless based upon similar preconceptions. Well over a third of the writing (46 per cent) done as part of English by the classes he observed was fictional. Another 15 per cent was made up of personal accounts of one kind or another; only 10 per cent could be described as 'information', 'argument' or 'utilitarian' (Medway, 1986a). Among classes of older students, there proved to be a marked difference between the writing done by those sitting different examinations. Thirty per cent of the pieces written by students sitting a conventional examination paper were either fictional or personal, whereas the corresponding figure for those whose assessment was to be based on coursework was 73 per cent, well over two-thirds of the writing they were doing in English (Barnes *et al.*, 1984). Thus many pupils aged both 12 and 15 years were experiencing a version of English dominated by stories and personal modes of writing; or, to use Medway's formulation, by writing that 'demanded an aesthetic reading'.

One result of this domination of writing in English lessons by literary models is that much of it is based upon 'idealized knowledge'. A composition on the topic 'An Autumn Day', for example, would not be an account of real events that had happened to the writer, but would lay tacit claim to be in some way representative of the generic experience of autumn (Medway, 1986a). Here is part of a piece written by a 13-year-old (not from Medway's sample) about 'winter':

> Winter is cold and gloomy and everything around you seems to be cold and dark. But then Christmas comes and everything changes, no more long cold and lonely nights, and going sledging and getting wet and then sitting by the fire and trying to keep yourself warm. I always look forward to Christmas Eve. . . .

In writing of this kind the reference is not to experienced reality but to literary discourse: competence in it is not based on understanding of how the world is, but on familiarity with existing forms of literary writing. Nineteenth-century literature, of course, provides many sources of conventional images and sentiments suited to writing of this kind; these discourse types provide not only subject matter and incidents – we all know what 'winter' would be likely to include – but appropriate styles of language too. Much of the fictional writing too done by the younger secondary pupils was conventional – the ghost story, the visitor from outer space, and so on. The claim sometimes made by teachers that such writing exercises 'the imagination' is misleading, for it is more a matter of practising existing fictional modes with well-developed repertoires of structures, events and attitudes. Thus, for these younger pupils, learning to write meant to a considerable extent learning to operate an array of discourse types, both fictional and non-fictional. Another way of saying this is that they were learning ground rules, though it seems probable that their teachers were unaware of this when they 'taught writing'.

Ground rules in some lessons

About half of the writing lessons observed in the *Versions of English* study as part of fifth-year English courses fell into the category called 'personal'. This category included stories and autobiographical writing, and carried with it powerful implicit ground rules for what constituted an acceptable performance. Ground rules were implicit – and sometimes explicit – in many of the lessons observed, and in a later section we shall consider what the pupils were able to make of the teachers' messages. Many of the lessons illustrate well how the ground rules of literary writing are communicated to pupils. For some years, many English teachers have made it their practice to read a series of poems or prose extracts to pupils before requiring them to write: these extracts are usually related in subject matter to the topic proposed for the writing. In one lesson observed, a teacher first told his fifth-year pupils that he was 'wanting to tie language and literature up' and then introduced some readings by saying, 'What I want you to be thinking about in your next language assignment . . . is your own family life.' He went on to read a group of poems all taken from a section (called 'Family Life') of a widely used school anthology of poems. As in many other such collections, the poems were organized in 'themes', a form of ordering that appears to support the function that the poems were to have in this lesson, that of presenting implicitly a set of ground rules defining (at least in part) the kind of writing that the pupils were expected to do. One poem, called *My Sister*, had been written by a 14-year-old girl. After reading it aloud, the teacher pointed out how the writer had compared her sister to a cat, as he said, 'a technique of description to take one aspect of a person's personality and take it through, right through the description comparing every action, every mood with the animal . . .'. He then asked the class, 'Have you any feelings about your own sisters and brothers that are like that?', but (not surprisingly) they seemed reluctant to reply. Next, he read a poem called *Baking Day* in which the poet describes her mother at work; attention was directed to the detailed description of the mother's hand covered with dough. Next, Theodore Roethke's poem *My Papa's Waltz* was read, but not commented on: the account of the poet's father coming home lively with drink and whisking the child into a soundless waltz was left to speak for itself.

Most interesting of all was the prose passage, taken from another course book organized in themes, which was read last. This was the passage in *Sons and Lovers* in which Paul Morel takes Clara home to meet his mother. It is worth quoting the teacher's comments in full:

> Thing I want you to notice in that passage, and you could try and capture it if you write something similar as part of your assignment, is the way in which the people in it think that they know what the other person is thinking but really they don't. Mrs Morel is sitting there weighing Clara up and thinking, 'I can sort her out; I'm stronger than her; she's no trouble'. And Clara's thinking, 'I expected something hard and cold, but she's quite a nice little woman really when she's chatting'. And Paul's thinking, 'They're going to get on very well together', and he doesn't see what's underneath it.

It is no mean feat to express the implications of a scene such as this so clearly as to make them available to 15-year-olds. It is because this teacher is unusually articulate that his presentation can be used to demonstrate meanings transmitted more vaguely by others.

By reading this passage and the poems to his pupils he is seeking to communicate a model of the kind of writing that he is wanting from them, at least in the piece of writing being prepared during that lesson. That is, he is seeking to communicate the criteria appropriate to writing about people and their relationships in a particular way, the ground rules of a particular mode of discourse. What he is recommending to them are essentially the sensibilities – the ways of seeing and feeling – appropriate to the novelist and poet, and along with them appropriate skills and modes of writing. He underlines the choice of details, the expression of feeling, and the choice of metaphors, as well as the novelist's ability to express ironical contrasts within a scene. At the same time, he is implicitly recommending choice of subject matter: what he values is sensitivity in face-to-face, particularly domestic, relationships, and insight into people's perspectives and motives. Most readers of this chapter will have been brought up in a cultural tradition – including notably the nineteenth-century English novel – that has rendered such assumptions normal, yet they are only one set of possible ways of perceiving and communicating experience. English, in this lesson, is coterminous with presenting this cultural tradition to the pupils.

We have chosen to focus closely upon this lesson, yet it has characteristics in common with many other such lessons taught in preparation for public examinations in English language. The choice of the word 'language' is not a slip of the pen: here the literature has become a vehicle for the transmission of the ground rules of a model of writing. Typically, in such an introduction to a writing task, the poems or prose passages are read aloud, but they are unlikely to be read closely: the teacher will not make use of the methodology of literary criticism in order to help the pupils to analyse them. The procedures of a 'literature' lesson would be quite different, and they would embody a different set of expectations for the eventual writing. In preparing for writing in 'language', the purpose of reading the extracts is to propose a subject matter, and to imply not only a way of writing about the subject, but at the same time a set of priorities and perceptions about people's lives. That is, these ground rules highlight certain aspects of our lives and propose a way of understanding them. They implicitly represent the teacher's expectations for that piece of writing, but lying half-hidden behind these particular expectations there are general ground rules that may be more important, partly because they are even less explicit. The lesson that we have used as an example is especially interesting in that it contains two sets of ground rules: by directing attention to the way in which, for example, one of the poems was constructed, the teacher was pointing towards a more deliberate *belles lettres* mode of writing, while the personal experience mode was implicit throughout in the way his comments focused upon the minutiae of interpersonal relationships.

An important part of the ground rules referred to what constituted acceptable content. One typical lesson was intended to prepare the class of 15- and 16-year-olds for writing about their earliest remembered experiences, a typical focus for 'personal' writing. In the course of the lesson, both the teacher and the pupils told anecdotes from their earliest years, and discussed some of the issues arising from them. Although these discussions implied an interest in pupils' reflections on their experiences, such reflections seldom appeared explicitly in the eventual writings, even though the teacher would probably have valued this. The issues discussed during this lesson included:

- first day at school;
- a child's relationship with an adult;
- childhood fantasies and punishment;
- the advisability of compelling children to eat food;
- children being lost by their parents;
- children as judges of character;
- the effects on children of parents' quarrels;
- tolerance for people who are different;
- how to bring up children; and
- gender roles.

Although this collection of topics strongly reflects the priorities and values of a particular teacher, it also well represents the kind of interests expected to characterize 'personal' writing. The writer is expected to reflect on his or her first-hand experience and find in it material that can be interestingly shared with others. The prime focus is upon the subjective qualities of experience, and particularly on representing face-to-face relationships and those involving family and other intimates.

Other characteristics are common in such writing. The lessons concerned with 'personal writing' were analysed to find what they had in common. All contained at least two of the following, and some contained all five:

- the reading of literary passages as an introduction to the topic;
- the telling of anecdotes;
- the urging of pupils to express feelings;
- an indication that narrative treatment of the topic will be acceptable; and
- the transmission of values by the teacher.

Several of the teachers also urged their pupils to include realistic details in their writing so as to make the reader able to imagine the experience as it was. It was interesting to notice that this advice had been effective enough for a number of pupils to mention this when they were talking about good writing. However, the advice makes the matter seem more simple than it is: the choice of appropriate details, and their formulation in words, requires particularly literary sensitivities. Success depends upon these much more than upon looking into one's heart.

What we have here is a powerful set of messages about this kind of writing. Not only is first-hand experience important, but it is to be presented in a way that communicates what it felt like, and how the writer at present sees it, including some expression of values. The whole adds up to an expectation that many topics will be dealt with in a predominantly literary manner, with the kind of realistic detail common in many nineteenth-century novels. An examination of the writing done during and after these lessons shows that the topics often appeared to be general and related to larger public issues, such as violence or old age or war. It was noticeable, however, that these were frequently dealt with in a highly personalized manner, often through narrative: *War*, for example, might turn into a set of imaginary letters written to his wife by a soldier in the front line during the 1914–18 war; *Vandalism* may be represented by a first-person account of an imaginary incident. Thus what appears superficially – perhaps in an examination paper or a list of essay topics – to be an invitation to write about a general issue, turns out to be literary writing that transmutes the general issues into personal experiences. Here a younger pupil is turning the unpromising topic 'Winter' into an occasion for quasi-autobiographical fiction:

> I kicked the pile of snow at the bottom of the garden, I was angry. I mean it wasn't even my fault. I can't stand Ralph, I can't stand the lot of them. It all started when me, Ralph and the lads stood at the street corner of Roydstone Terrace telling each other what we were going to get for Christmas . . .

Making general issues personal clearly has its advantages, but if it becomes normal it can trivialize them by making only face-to-face relationships seem important.

Our purpose here is not necessarily to question the value of autobiographical and fictional writing; the ability to use language to explore personal experience is an important part of the school curriculum. Our point is rather that a central part of what was learnt in these lessons was a set of requirements that were only partly made explicit by the teachers, and which even older secondary pupils found hard to talk about. Other lessons did require other kinds of writing, though these were a small proportion of the whole writing done in English even by 16-year-olds. One might have expected some comparative discussion of different kinds of writing and their respective functions and characteristics, but this occurred in only one of all the classrooms observed during the *Versions of English* study.

So far, our comments have referred almost entirely to narrative, autobiographical and reflective writing. The writing of verse and of play scripts does take place, but because this too is literary it does not require a separate commentary. Not all of the topics set for pupils to write about are obviously 'personal/literary': an analysis of titles set by teachers showed that 38 per cent of them appeared to invite discussion of a public issue (Barnes *et al.*, 1984). However, these were frequently interpreted by pupils – with or without the encouragement of their teachers – to be invitations to write fiction, or semi-fiction of an autobiographical kind. The proportion of essays actually written in a 'public' manner with some engagement in general discussion varied from 10 to 16 per cent.

The content of writing

We now turn to the relationships of writing in English lessons to the pupils' experiences in the world outside school. Much of the writing done by 12-year-olds amounted to 'a decorous display of appropriate conventional sentiments': it did not require them to understand their own lives but rather to conform to the ground rules of various conventional literary genres by 'recycling book knowledge' (Medway, 1986b).

It is worth asking at this point why young people should not learn to write through gaining mastery of existing genres, by accepting the order already available in existing fictional worlds. After all, young people throughout history have begun their development through gaining access to the taken-for-granted activities and meanings of adult culture. Despite teachers' claims that any topics could be dealt with, the range of topics in their pupils' writing proved to be limited. In the first place, they were constrained by the expectation that most of them would deal with people's relationships within their immediate social world with particular attention to 'emotionally charged personal situations' and the 'ordering of the feelings' through literary means. What was valued was an ability to 'make experience real', the creation of the literary effect, ideally through 'a Wordsworthian freshness of vision'.

The predominance of this kind of writing in English lessons seems to carry an implicit message that reality is located solely in inner experience. Much of the writing, whether or not explicitly fictional, deals with the more intense moments of personal experience – the family quarrel, the realization of loss and loneliness, the experience of young lovers, episodes of violence – with particular focus upon interpersonal relationships and their effects. Important though these moments are in our lives, they certainly do not constitute the whole.

As a result of this, the writers' efforts were mainly directed to creating a sense of verisimilitude, concerned more with representing the world than with acting upon it. (This seems analogous to the preference for 'poetic' rather than 'transactional' writing expressed in the work of the London Writing Research Unit of the 1970s: Britton *et al.*, 1975.) Whole areas of experience were being ignored:

> Young people notice the police officer next door getting into a big new car, the corner shop going over to video hire, the deteriorating health of the woman down the road, the change in the threshold of acceptable language in television soap operas, the formation of a community group to fight the closure of a school or the opening of a hostel for the mentally handicapped, the new graffiti on the wall of the Sikh temple, the sudden change in the dress and demeanour of a friend's mother, the appearance on the lampposts of small posters in Arabic, the adoption by a local teenager of a form of fundamentalist Christianity, the difference made to the man across the road by his new hip, and the still empty factory unit in the field where they used to play. (Medway, 1988)

Of course, it is not merely the omission of such topics that is to be regretted, but the ground rules for living that may be implicit in the omission.

A writing curriculum based only upon idealized knowledge drawn from literature fails to encourage speculation and curiosity and takes little or no account of those wider social forces and pressures that shape young people's future lives. In the writing of 12-year-olds, there was 'a lack of generalizing and analysing', its place being taken by narration and that strangely artificial school activity called 'writing a description' (Medway, 1986b). Young people were being given little encouragement to use writing as an opportunity to find and develop significance in their own experiences. (Some are all too ready to find everyday life shapeless and uninteresting, or at least irrelevant to school.)

We share with many English teachers the belief that in speech as well as in writing we are able to restructure our perceptions of the world, though this restructuring depends upon access to cultural resources that are shared with others and thus sometimes reinforced and sometimes challenged. But the writing tasks we have described tell pupils implicitly that they should accept the order already available in fictional worlds rather than learn how to find patterns of meaning in their own experiences (Medway, 1986b). The writing curriculum in English lessons is thus failing to help pupils to 'interrogate the world', to take a critical and inquiring attitude to the life about them, mainly because of its concentration upon the ideal knowledge provided by literature. Not only that: most of the writing done in schools is essentially contemplative; it narrates, describes, analyses and explains, not only in English but in other subjects too. Yet in the world outside school most writing is concerned to make something happen, to influence or to plan or to set up a critique.

Ground rules for writing are important not merely because pupils have to master them in order to do well in school, but because they are often ground rules for living too. There is good reason to argue that the school curriculum should – among its other functions – help young people to make their social environment the object of conscious attention, and to develop an enquiring and critical attitude to it. Writing is part of social action: for most adults the writing they do is part of their active engagement in living. It is seldom merely contemplative. The English curriculum in most secondary schools has failed to realize its potential to help pupils to interrogate the world about them. (The version of English incorporated in the National Curriculum is no more helpful in this.) All of education should help young people to question the world's appearances and understand how it comes to be as it is, or to learn how to influence it.

At an earlier point in this chapter we looked at the way in which two teachers made some of their ground rules available to those pupils able to grasp them. It is now appropriate to consider what sense most pupils make of the messages about ground rules that come their way, often from teachers less skilful than those two. When pupils of 15 or 16 years of age were interviewed about their work in English, many of them talked about improving their writing, and what would be required to achieve this (Barnes *et al.*, 1984). Their teachers will undoubtedly have tried to communicate what kinds of writing they value, so that when their pupils talked about good writing this threw light upon which of those messages had been understood. The number of times that various characteristics of 'good writing' were mentioned by pupils are summarized below. The more superficial aspects have been separated from those that were concerned with the content and its expression.

Surface

Orthographic conventions	26	
Neatness	13	52
Vocabulary and sentence structure	13	

Deep

Content	15	
Thought	9	32
Expression	8	

It was something of a surprise to find that so many students of this age, just about to complete compulsory schooling, were still placing such a major emphasis – nearly 40 per cent of all the references – on spelling, punctuation and neatness. This may reflect the values of the community outside schools rather than those of the teachers: one girl said that even though the teacher had been urging her to think more about what she wrote, she knew that it was really 'neatness that matters'. There may still be contexts in which that is so, but for most writing it seems inappropriate as a major criterion.

Both teacher and taught are faced with the undoubted difficulty of talking explicitly about deep criteria. When pupils talked about the content of their writing, perhaps two-thirds of them mentioned 'having a good idea'; such 'ideas', however, seemed more often to refer to original ways of handling a story than to lines of thought appropriate to discursive essays. A few pupils were more explicit: one who said that she often 'lacked ideas' went on to characterize these as 'an everyday sort of knowledge'. Other pupils spoke of the importance of knowledge of people and experiences from life, but these few were exceptionally articulate young people. Some of the nine references to 'thought' were probably not very different from 'ideas'. Many pupils had been told that they ought to plan their writing in advance and had a vaguely guilty feeling about not doing so. Style and expression tended to be spoken about in an equally vague way.

Because they had written mainly fictional and personal pieces, it was not surprising that only a small proportion of the pupils mentioned the need to present opinions and to find arguments and evidence to support them. These interviews threw light upon some of the unspoken expectations that lay beneath what the pupils were able to make explicit. Despite the anxieties expressed in some sections of the Press, these young people were very concerned about surface criteria such as neatness, spelling and punctuation; and when they mentioned deep criteria, what they said suggested that for them writing in English was predominantly personal and literary.

Ground rules and examinations

So far we have been taking what teachers say in lessons and what pupils have said in interviews as our primary sources of information about what constitutes the ground rules for writing in English lessons. Most secondary teachers are not free agents; they must measure their success by their pupils' examination results, however much they are also influenced by other values. For this reason, examination papers provide an alternative source of ground rules. But examination papers do not speak for themselves; what reaches the pupils comes to them by courtesy of what their teachers tell them about how to work for examinations, including how to manage writing tasks set under formal examination conditions and what kinds of coursework should be written for inclusion in the folders of work to be assessed. In spite of this, much can be learnt directly from examination papers, as teachers both shape examination norms – through membership of examination committees, for example – and are shaped by them during years of working within their demands. This is not to say that there are no differences from one teacher to another or that there are no teachers who transmit idiosyncratic expectations to their pupils. (Examiners' mark schemes can also be highly informative about their ground rules, though these are not often made public.)

We can thus expect that examination papers in English language will embody implicit models of what writing should be for pupils at the end of compulsory schooling. Papers in English literature can be expected to display a more specialized conception of a proper way, or ways, of writing about works of literature. That is, examination papers constitute a practical means of defining for teachers and learners alike what constitutes 'writing' for their current purposes, a definition all the more powerful as it is directly related to certification and to competition for jobs. The implicit ground rules, here and in all other subjects, define what must be done in order to be 'a good student'.

Writing tasks in English language examinations differ from one another in the extent to which the examiners lay down explicit requirements or apparently leave the choice to the candidate. These requirements include indications of what content is expected, and the mode or genre of the writing. The starting points that examiners present to the candidates vary sharply in their explicitness: some are no more than a word or a phrase for the candidate to interpret – 'Bargains' or 'Making Up' for example. Others can be even less sharply defined: there may be a photograph of an old person or an evocative description in prose or verse of a thunderstorm. In either case, the candidate must choose how to respond, though the prose or verse would probably carry implicit messages about the style to be adopted. (Such starting points are analogous to lessons in which writing is introduced by the reading of passages of literature.) Other writing tasks provide much more explicit instructions:

> We can learn a lot about people from the way they dress. Write about the suitability
> of various types of clothing for work and leisure, and explain why, in your opinion,
> so much importance is often attached to people's outward appearance.

Examiners set tasks like these, no doubt, with the intention of supplying pointers to appropriate content, perhaps in the hope that the resulting assessment will depend less upon the candidates' knowledge and more upon their ability as writers (if the two can be said to exist separately). This formulation suggests to candidates that they might deal not with clothing as a whole but should consider clothes for different purposes, and that other matters such as dress as a signal of status or personality might be included. (The reader may have noted also the parenthesis 'in your opinion', which suggests that the examiners were aware of one of the ground rules that we discussed in Chapter 1.)

The more explicit tasks attempt to shift the emphasis away from the generation of content by giving suggestions to all candidates alike, thus freeing them from the possible disadvantages of not having ready access to those ground rules that govern appropriateness of content. In contrast, the more 'open' or implicit tasks treat the generation of a range of ideas as the business of the candidate, with the result that the content of the essay – the ideas generated by the writer – carries much more weight in the final assessment.

Indications of the expected mode of writing vary similarly. In some tasks, the genre or style of writing is constrained by explicit instructions, but in others the candidate is apparently free to choose. For example, the topic 'Making Up' could lead to the writing of a story, an idealized descriptive account, an autobiographical passage, or a reflective piece on sincerity, or the contrast between appearance and reality. The freedom to choose, however, is qualified by the fact that any choice is open to evaluation by unknown assessors who are using invisible ground rules that the candidate flouts at his or her peril.

These contrasts in explicitness can be illustrated by two pairs of questions drawn from an analysis carried out a few years ago of writing tasks in GCE and CSE English language papers.

> *GCE:* Do the British run themselves down too much? What things can we be proud of?
>
> *CSE:* An American pen-friend who has never visited England and who knows nothing about the country apart from what he or she has read in the press or seen on television, asks you what it is like to be a young man or young woman growing up here. . . . Write the reply you would send.
>
> *GCE:* What attracts people to clubs and societies? What is your own attitude to group activities?
>
> *CSE:* You have started a new club at your school. Write an article for the school magazine giving details of the activities of your club and trying to persuade other pupils to join. (Barnes and Seed, 1984)

These pairs illustrate well two sets of contrasting ground rules:

> In such cases the contrast is palpable between: a brief open-ended question versus more detailed instruction and a delimited form; intellectual, abstract debate versus a personal, persuasive, concrete account; a self-sufficient and autonomous discourse versus a social 'occasion'. (Barnes and Seed, 1984)

We have no wish to establish a preference for detailed rather than open-ended questions, or of analytical rather than personalized writing. Our interest in these writing tasks from previous examinations lies in the fact that they not only embody ground rules but appear to offer different ground rules to different groups of pupils – those entered for CSE as against those entered for the more prestigious GCE. The less explicit writing tasks either assume that all students are equally conversant with the unstated norms and expectations, or are in effect including knowledge of those norms among the abilities that are being tested. The latter is more likely, because those candidates who are unable to intuit what will seem appropriate to the assessors are very likely to be penalized, not for disobeying instructions but rather because the apparent inappropriateness of what they write will seem unintelligent, or unbalanced, or lacking in stylistic tact.

In setting the more explicit tasks, the examiners seem to have said to themselves: 'Not all pupils have access to these public modes, or to the implicit values that underlie choices of content or style, so we will choose writing tasks which since they are close to everyone's daily concerns will give opportunity to all to show their language abilities.' (Barnes and Seed, 1984) But in supplying a common content for the writing the examiners fell into the trap of stereotyping 'ordinary boys' and girls' lives and interests'. Because the tasks included quite specific assumptions about the social and cultural life of the candidates, their ability to project themselves into these stereotypes became part of what was tested:

> The pertinent question as far as examination papers are concerned is how far their questions veto certain kinds of experience and language and thus make certain cultural traits a disqualification. (Barnes and Seed, 1984)

In the papers analysed, these stereotypes proved to be of two kinds. Many of the writing tasks were judged to 'project a stereotyped and inappropriate social ethos – a stable nuclear family (the Janet and John syndrome) or the traditional grammar school culture – or subtly suggest a particular moralised version of behaviour'. The phrase 'traditional grammar school culture' refers to questions that assumed that the school's life was made up of 'speech days and head boys, pupil clubs and societies, pen pals, school magazines'. Questions that require candidates to write about how they would spend money or use leisure time may carry unspoken values incommensurate with the real way of life of many pupils. The second stereotype provided a picture of everyday urban life as the examiners believed young people were experiencing it: 'a world of domestic experience . . . of the family, the peer group, the club, at worst a kind of parody of urban working class life' (Barnes and Seed, 1984).

To succeed in writing built upon such stereotypes often requires pupils to pretend to live in a world not their own, and to ape attitudes and activities that they have not experienced at first hand:

> When pupils are forced to project themselves into an alien situation the weakness of the resulting writing may not stem from a lack of communication ability but from a socially induced incomprehension of the appropriate codes.

Ground rules may become barriers to school success.

Since that analysis was carried out, the General Certificate of Secondary Education (GCSE) has been substituted for GCE and CSE, so it is appropriate to consider whether that examination has brought any changes in the ground rules for writing in English language. In a sample of nine GCSE English language papers, it appeared that the brief essay title on a public topic has all but disappeared. In several of the papers highly explicit instructions were given, providing content for the writing, more explicit definition of what is required and, in many cases, an imaginary context to which the writing would relate. The provision of quotations, often lengthy, as a starting point for writing has become standard practice, about half being literary. The emphasis upon first-hand interpersonal experience remains prominent, but for most examination boards it is balanced by a contrasting mode of writing that deals with material from the public domain and seeks, with limited success, to imitate realistic tasks in realistic contexts. (The organization of a marathon race, the Channel Tunnel, extracts from guidebooks, and an extraordinary eight-page collection of articles, extracts, statistical charts and pictures all referring to gender issues.) Examiners seem to conceive of two contrasting kinds of writing called 'Argumentative and Informative Writing' or 'Personal and Expressive Writing', a dichotomy that fails to reflect the immense subtlety with which writers can adjust to varying purposes and contexts, or the range of strategies that even 16-year-olds can generate.

The expected mode of writing is still predominantly personal and literary, so that most candidates will be writing stories or autobiographical pieces, such as 'an occasion when you sulked or felt angry' or 'being an only child'. Literary criteria still sometimes linger even in the more public pieces of writing. For example, when in one paper the candidates were asked to write an article for a local newspaper about a man who ran in the London marathon, the examiners were instructed to give the highest marks to candidates who 'bring alive the character of Mr B. . . , the impact of the marathon as an event, and . . . build sympathy for the handicapped people involved'.

The attempt to relate some of the writing tasks more closely to the public purposes for which adults write creates a problem for examination boards, for how can real-life purposes and contexts be brought into an examination room? The imaginary contexts proposed to the candidates are not always very persuasive, being dominated by letters to local newspapers, talks to other fifth formers, articles for school magazines, and leaflets for imaginary purposes. (A not untypical requirement was to write 'a paragraph for your friends' about a place of historical importance – based on extracts from three guidebooks – and also to make a plan for a school visit to the resort.) These pretend contexts do not alter the fact that the candidates are writing to please unseen examiners. It is not certain that such imaginary contexts are of service to the young people sitting the examination. As we have suggested, candidates often have as a result to penetrate the assumptions of alien and unrealistic cultural milieux. The attempt to move towards public writing is marred by the artificiality of these imaginary contexts, yet it is difficult to see how the tasks could be made more realistic within the bounds of a conventional examination paper. At least one GCSE syllabus is assessed entirely through coursework, which opens the possibility of writing for more realistic purposes and audiences, though it seems all too likely (1990) that the government will ban such syllabuses.

There has clearly been a shift in the implicit ground rules that young people have to master in order to succeed. They now have to manage two contrasting modes, and pick up clues from the papers about the styles and characteristics that will be valued. They have been largely released from the problem of selecting suitable material, and from the need to adopt the Olympian style of balanced discussion required by the traditional essay. Nevertheless, in English they will still have to penetrate the ground rules for personal/literary writing and the stylistic requirements hidden in that apparently innocuous requirement to draft a pamphlet or write a letter. But that is what 'English' is.

Ground rules in writing about literature

The ground rules that characterize writing about English literature differ from those in lessons devoted to 'language work'; we shall deal with them only briefly. Conventions about how to analyse works of literature take a central place, and include ideas such as 'character', 'theme' and 'plot'. These are so familiar that we forget that they are not necessary or universal, for they are no more than conventional ways of breaking down the experience of reading literature in order to talk and write about it. Why 'character'? Do we all really read novels and watch plays as if we were meeting real people? Does a traditional 'character sketch' always reflect the way in which we understand and respond to a work of literature? Questions about characters, which still survive in literature examinations, are based upon similar assumptions about verisimilitude to those so effectively criticized by L. C. Knights many years ago in his 'How many children had Lady Macbeth?' To read a story or watch a play as if it dealt with real people and events is often very misleading. Similarly, with 'plot'. Although this at least acknowledges that a work of art is an artefact, it does not always provide a valid way of thinking about the construction of a novel or play. Nearly a third of the questions in a sample of English literature papers referred to 'character' and more than a third required discussion of a 'theme' extracted from the work (Barnes and Seed, 1984). The only other substantial category was made up of questions requiring the narration of some aspect of the story.

The style of writing expected in a literature essay is also different. Pupils are expected to display an 'appropriate response' to a text, that is, they are expected to show that they have understood it in an acceptable way, but they would also be expected to conform to certain conventions about how one writes about works of literature. At a trivial level this includes superficialities of style: one chief examiner at A-level made a point in his annual report of criticizing a candidate who wrote, 'It was all up with Lear who couldn't take any more of it'. We can find no fault with the meaning of this assertion; the manner must have been thought to lack decorum. English literature defends the decorum of its discourse as energetically as any of the sciences.

It has already been observed that such principles as the need to support assertions with evidence or arguments very seldom figured in what pupils said about writing in English *language* because of the dominance of literary ground rules. Ironically, it is likely to be in writing about *literary* topics that these principles do appear, for English teachers repeatedly urge their pupils to support their statements with 'references to the text'. They also talk about 'making points' in literature essays, and are concerned about the sequence of ideas. This contrasts sharply with the intuitivist assumptions that often characterize the setting of writing tasks labelled 'English language'.

The teaching of ground rules

It seems inevitable that the reader – whether or not a teacher of English – will respond to this descriptive account of the ground rules effective in English courses by asking what should be done about it. It is not our intention to offer dogmatic recipes: the matter is far too complex for that, yet the challenge has to be met.

The term 'stimulus' has been used ever since the 1960s by English teachers when they talk about the starting-points for writing which they give to their pupils, though in their usage it has none of the implications of automatic responses that it had in its earlier use by psychologists. The English teachers' usage arose out of the realization that most young people write best when they have some control over the topic for writing and how they tackle it. A 'stimulus' was – and still is – a passage of prose, a poem, a picture or a piece of music intended to generate in the pupils an awareness of a range of possibilities for writing, yet without narrowly defining a single focus. Thus it contrasts with the older practice of presenting pupils with a mere title (such as 'Bridges') to make something of. The stimulus is expected to encourage the writers to select a topic and approach that makes sense to them, because good writing is held to come from the emerging purposes of the individual writer. This account of writing has much to recommend it, yet it fails to tell the whole story.

The idea of 'stimulus' seems to imply that writing comes naturally to those who find a purpose. 'Fool', said my Muse to me, 'Look in thy heart and write'; Sir Philip Sidney has much to answer for. The skill and deliberate planning required by many kinds of writing have been undervalued in the interests of direct outpourings in which the writer is writing primarily for him or herself. This kind of writing – intended for no one else but the sympathetic eye of the English teacher – is treated as the norm.

Thus English teaching since the 1950s has been based upon a tacit intuitivism, which has turned away from any attempt to make techniques and criteria of writing explicit. Originally, this suspicion of ground rules was based on a well-justified rejection of previous methods of teaching writing through practice in forming words, sentences and paragraphs, methods that were demonstrably unhelpful. However, it can be argued that it is time that this suspicion of explicit analysis was abandoned in favour of helping older pupils to become conscious of what is involved in good writing of various kinds.

Much writing is not straightforward expression from the heart, even much literary writing. Elsewhere in the curriculum, writing is almost always to fulfil someone else's purposes, and for much of the time in English too. However sincere English teachers are in asserting that their pupils are writing for themselves, English as much as any other school subject takes place in a context of assessment. Most writing in secondary schools is for someone else to evaluate, and many pupils are indignant if they do not receive some evaluative feedback. Moreover, much of what older secondary pupils write in English is intended for examination folders. As a result, it is as important for pupils to have access to the values and expectations of English teachers as of any other subject. Even when the English teacher is urging the pupils to explore their experience and to choose topics and approaches that are important to them, the pupils know that they must nevertheless attend to unspoken requirements for appropriateness. The truth is that pupils are still constrained by adult expectations; they must learn how to make their interests and experience acceptable, and what must be omitted. They must learn too the ground rules of the personal/literary modes in which to represent that experience. Despite the rhetoric of 'writing for oneself' and the obsession with authenticity, it is the exceptional pupils who can make school writing at the same time serve their own purposes and meet the teacher's – and the unseen examiner's – ground rules.

The assumption that it is not necessary to teach writing seems to arise from the belief that pupils are expressing their own feelings directly, without the mediation of those cultural systems that we are calling ground rules. There are three ways in which ground rules may be made more available to adolescents: there can be more explicit discussion of the requirements of particular kinds of writing whenever the pupils embark on them; there can be an extension of literary critical discussion to include an understanding of the cultural norms implicit in texts of various kinds; and there can be more direct teaching of how to write in various modes.

Reading and writing should be taught in tandem: preparation for writing about, for example, 'Finding a job', might include the reading of a series of passages that included autobiographical and fictional approaches, but also general discussion of social as well as economic aspects of employment and unemployment, and even passages mainly concerned with presenting information. The teaching would deal not only with their surface differences as texts but with the way in which the differences of content, structure and style relate both to the nature of the material and purposes of the writer and to the context for which they are intended. The purposes, open and covert, of the writers would be looked at, as well as the likely effect on particular readers. Texts would not be treated as an unbroken continuum, or in terms of the neat 'expressive/informational' dichotomy that we found in GCSE papers, but examined for what they were and what they aspired to be in the contexts for which they were intended.

Both as readers and writers, all pupils need to learn interpretive strategies appropriate to particular audiences, situations and purposes, but this has not so far been a strong element in English teaching. This is why pupils' reading and writing should encompass a wider range of genres than has been prescribed by the personal/literary tradition of recent years, for it is during the discussion of the reading and writing that the necessary perceptions and preferences can be implicitly as well as explicitly communicated. In sum, for older pupils writing should be embedded in a study of discourse – the uses of language in relation to the dynamics of its social contexts.

More explicit teaching of writing strategies will also be needed. The requirements of GCSE must already have brought some changes in the balance of writing done in examination classes for English. There is every reason to help pupils to develop more effective strategies for composition, particularly outside the personal modes. Asking them to write an outline in advance is ineffective: it requires them to solve all of their problems before they have begun to work on them. Ways of accumulating and organizing ideas can be taught, however. The current advocacy of redrafting is healthy, but it should be remembered that for practised writers it is the redrafting that takes place during drafting that is most important, for that is how the writer works through his or her changing conception of what the finished piece will be like as it develops on the page. Most pupils need help during drafting to look at what they have written so far and consider whether it is going in the required direction: this does not come by nature.

Nevertheless, there are limits to what can be taught and learnt through explicit instruction. Much of our social learning comes from participating in activities with other people who are operating ground rules: if we become aware of the 'rules' it is usually somewhat later when some unusual incident forces us to reflect. For this reason, feedback from teachers and even from other pupils would be very important. Most English teachers have decided that a mark and brief comment on pupils' work is not enough, and try as often as possible to talk individually to them. Such advice about writing in progress is far more valuable than that given before or after. Other pupils, too, have an important role, but would need careful preparation to enable them to act as critical readers giving feedback *inter alia* about their classmates' failures to respond to unspoken ground rules (though that is not how they would put it).

No doubt new sets of ground rules are emerging: the presence in GCSE papers of tasks of a more public nature shows one direction of change. Some English teachers now believe that their older pupils should engage in writing designed to engage with the world outside school and perhaps even try to change it. This includes offering to provide writing services to persons and organizations as well as gathering information in order to contribute in writing to a public debate. These new purposes and contexts for writing need to be discussed explicitly with pupils so that they understand the requirements of the tasks they are undertaking. Pupils can only gain from becoming aware of the considerations that an experienced adult writer would be taking into account, even though we must keep in mind that the choices in the actual writing are so complex that many of them must be taken without conscious thought.

5 Conclusion

Disciplined thinking and writing

Throughout this book we have used the concept of ground rules to help us to understand the taken-for-granted thinking processes that underlie teaching and learning in various secondary school subjects. In the earlier chapters we have attempted to show that specialist subjects consist of collections of both implicit and explicit rules and organizing principles governing both academic cognition and the social presentation of knowledge in the form of writing. Within the specialist subject classroom, children may be required to perform a variety of intellectual and social tasks, each with their particular set of ground rules or frameworks. Different constellations or configurations of ground rules will thus make up each one of the different school subjects in the experience of the child. This is their perceived reality of 'doing history' or 'doing science' in school.

How does the child's experience of school subjects relate to the concept of disciplines and disciplined thinking held by adults? In their own education and training, most teachers have encountered three main approaches to the curriculum, all of which make large (and often unreflective) assumptions about the nature of school subjects. 'Traditional' teachers favour a curriculum that is taught in a framework of separate subjects. They see each of the disciplines as having distinctively different characteristics and offering unique insights. The primary purpose of education is seen by such teachers as induction into the intellectual conventions of a particular community of scholars. 'Progressive' teachers, on the other hand, tend to favour a curriculum that is based upon project work and may take one of two positions about the place and value of the disciplines. Some believe that the insights from various disciplines can be used to inform their pupils' thinking about certain aspects of the topic being studied, even though no discipline can provide an overall structure of learning. For such teachers, the disciplines serve primarily as a means to an end, the understanding of specific issues. Other progressive teachers may believe that there are really no distinctively different forms of knowledge, and that the disciplines that dominate secondary school curricula are artificial constructs that constrict and inhibit children's learning by making it very unlike the concerns that shape their lives. In the paragraphs that follow, we hope to explore some of the issues in this important controversy and to clarify some of the main issues that relate to 'disciplined' thinking by building on the conclusions reached in the earlier chapters.

In the field of educational theory, the views of the nature of subjects held by some philosophers and the views of some sociologists have polarized in a way that partly mirrors the more informal views of traditional and progressive teachers. The philosophers Hirst and Peters (1970) present the view that there are seven distinctively different forms of knowledge. Each is characterized by particular conceptual schemes and by unique ways of determining the truth of an assertion. These are the fundamental forms of knowledge; any other subjects or fields of study are a combination of insights drawn from these seven forms and applied to a particular area of study. This analysis is often misrepresented in popular educational literature as suggesting that the forms of knowledge are absolute and unchangeable. Hirst (1974) himself was quick to point out that this was not in fact the case:

> I am not suggesting that the fundamental categories of knowledge are anything other than the product of man's form of life, and nothing dogmatic is being asserted about their immutability or universality.

Nevertheless, Hirst and Peters's approach has largely fallen from favour, to be replaced by the currently popular sociological analysis of the disciplines as the outcomes of power struggles over careers and status in the academic world. This sociological analysis tends both to misrepresent the philosophers' views and to redirect investigation of the nature of the disciplines into socio-historical study. At worst, it becomes a socio-historical study of academic in-fighting:

> It would seem that, far from being timeless statements of intrinsically worthwhile content, subjects and disciplines are in constant flux. Hence the study of knowledge in our society should move beyond the ahistorical process of philosophical analysis towards a detailed historical investigation of the motives and actions behind the presentation and promotion of subjects and disciplines. (Goodson, 1988, p. 165)

We take the view that the work we have been engaged in can help to enlarge the debate by considering both cognitive and communicative aspects of disciplined thinking. If we use the concept of ground rules as a way of understanding how we think, it becomes increasingly difficult to conceive of a 'subject perspective' as a single, coherent and unproblematic conceptual framework through which to view any field of enquiry. This means that the position taken by Hirst and Peters underemphasizes the complex nature of what constitutes a discipline.

Hirst (1974) presents the school curriculum (in so far as it is based on the forms of knowledge) as made up of subjects each of which is homogeneous, logically coherent, based upon a common set of concepts and cognitive procedures, and made up of propositions that are capable of being disproved ('falsified' in his terminology). Each subject can offer warranted assertions about some aspect of the world, and the truth of these assertions is independent of the identity and motives of the person who utters them or the context in which they are made. As a result, every learner must submit to the requirements of the form of knowledge; his or her ability to learn depends upon successful induction into the system. Our view is that this picture of school subjects is so idealized as partly to misrepresent the nature of schooling. Subjects are not made up solely of propositional knowledge, but include values and priorities, rule-of-thumb procedures and interpretive ground rules that are just as essential to the subject as are the propositions. To describe subjects as propositions without ground rules is to misrepresent both how researchers collaborate in developing new meanings, and the needs of learners who wish to participate in the thinking of an existing discipline. Nor are subjects unvarying monoliths, as any pupil knows who has been taught biology by Miss X in one year and by Mr Y in the next.

We do not wish to misrepresent the view of knowledge presented by Peters and Hirst, or to fall into the trap of those sociologists who have become so interested in the idea of academic subjects as institutions as almost to forget that they are also attempts to understand the world. Research in the sociology of knowledge is right to emphasize that our traditional academic subjects are man-made rather than given. We share the view that each distinctive realm or domain of knowledge has its origin in a particular socio-historical setting and goes through changes over time. We would add to this, however, that social and cultural processes are involved in the development, consolidation and alteration of the interpretive frameworks and ground rules that are characteristic of our present forms of knowledge. And we would like to suggest that more than a power struggle among academics is at work shaping the characteristics of each discipline.

We certainly need to abandon, if we ever held it, the view of subjects as some immutable light upon truth. A more rounded understanding of their nature involves going beyond the current sociological analysis, because that tends to underplay the cognitive dimension. Disciplines arise as genuine attempts to understand particular aspects of the world we live in, and include the creation of shared frameworks for perception and interpretation of that world. They are sustained through the construction and reconstruction of meanings not only by teachers and academics but eventually by members of the public in their attempts to make use of the new constructs. Some sociological accounts seem to leave out the desire to understand some aspect of the world and to persuade others that one's account is acceptable. In order to persuade others, a writer has to adopt at least some of the taken-for-granted concepts, values and procedures that will be understood by fellow specialists. Thus success depends upon using the common stock of symbols to express meanings that diverge to a greater or lesser degree from what those symbols have traditionally signified.

This paradox has been discussed by Kuhn (1970), who, writing about revolutions in scientific theory, proposed the idea of guiding paradigms as a characteristic of science. In Kuhn's view, science was defined by shared commitment to particular theoretical, conceptual and methodological frameworks, which at some point might be overturned in favour of revolutionary new insights. Such an analysis is capable of incorporating the arguments of both Hirst and Goodson. Like Hirst and Peters, Kuhn is talking about conceptual schemes and truth criteria. But he also treats as part of science the kinds of interpretive schemes and cognitive and social ground rules that we have discussed in the earlier chapters. He confronts directly the issue of 'ways of seeing' and not just career and power struggles to explain the emergence of different subjects. Kuhn's analysis is therefore a broader and more subtle one, which gives due weight to the place of conceptual issues as definers of a discipline.

Kuhn describes as 'normal science' any work that explores the implications of the current theoretical paradigm, extending its meaning and applications without challenging it in any depth. What he calls a 'revolution' occurs only when the repair work on an ageing paradigm becomes so unconvincing that a new paradigm can be established in its place. (A familiar example is the supplanting of Newtonian physics by Einstein's relativity.) It is important to see the new paradigm not merely as a device by which a new group of scientists claim their place in the sun, but as at the same time a genuine attempt to describe the world more powerfully. (The use of the word 'powerfully' demands the question 'Powerfully for what purpose?', thus introducing complexities that cannot be addressed here.) The interlinking of 'normal science' and 'revolution', which cannot exist in separation, matches our conception of ground rules; the learner must learn to operate the ground rules in order to become a participant in the subject, but to accept them uncritically is to substitute authority for understanding.

We need, above all, to acknowledge the many cognitive and communicative ground rules that characterize the work of all groups of scholars working within whatever they define as their discipline. It appears that, at least in part, the disciplines we value so much are best seen as provisional methods for understanding the world around us. They have complex and changeable collections of ground rules moulded into distinctive conceptual frameworks for interpreting that world and writing about it. The conceptual frameworks cannot be understood without attending to the tacit ground rules that are needed to interpret them. By limiting his forms of knowledge to propositions, Hirst omitted this aspect of shared meanings, that they are never unambiguously available even to all those apparently qualified to use them, and certainly not to young people who are only just beginning to grasp how the frame can be used to understand the world.

In our education system, the provisional nature of knowledge has traditionally either been denied or revealed only to those who reach the stage of higher education, where the scales fall from their eyes during the course of reading for a degree. But there has been a growing movement advocating 'subversive teaching' (Postman and Weingartner, 1969) or 'critical thinking' (Brookfield, 1987). Advocates of critical thinking are conscious of the need to reveal underlying assumptions and to question habitual ways of thinking. And it is becoming increasingly common to argue that such an approach to learning should be part of every child's entitlement, integrated into their education from the start, to produce more reflective, independent-minded thinkers. Some ways of pursuing this objective are explored in the final section of this chapter.

The meaning of writing in school

In this section, we think it important to raise other issues related to writing, which none the less ultimately bear on the general theme of our conclusion; namely, the need to empower the learner through encouraging reflective thinking. The following discussion centres upon the act of producing writing and concerns the social function and meaning of writing in schools.

Our concern here is to show the interconnections between an everyday routine classroom activity and the wider social structure. There are a number of different ways in which the process and production of writing may serve to maintain existing social relationships. Very little has been written from a sociological point of view specifically about writing as a mechanism for socialization and social control. This is because, first, research on writing has usually been done by psychologists or teachers of English who have mainly focused on models of the writing process and on methods of developing writing competences, whereas sociologists have been more concerned with the face-to-face interactions of teachers and pupils. This has left an immense gap in the literature of the subject. We hope, therefore, that the following discussion will help to open up some debate in this area. We begin with an overview of some of the ways in which our understanding of writing in schools can be enhanced by such an approach, before focusing our attention more specifically on the way in which the analysis of ground rules can illuminate particular issues.

One important issue to consider is the difference between writing in school and writing in the world outside school, and the implications for teacher–pupil relationships. First, let us think about the function of what is written. Outside school, most people's writing serves an immediate practical purpose. We fill in forms, write letters, shopping lists and, possibly more reflectively, diaries and even stories and poems. People use writing to effect change, often as part of their jobs: they will prepare memoranda, instructions, reports, speeches, and so on. Yet others, those involved in providing education for others, will make notes, prepare lesson plans, write lectures, papers, dissertations and theses. But for the pupils in school, writing is often a far less directly purposeful activity. Instead, it is part of the daily routine of being in school, rarely needed to fulfil any real and immediate function, meaningful only in that it achieves a certain mark and gains the teacher's approval. To do well in one's written work is to display competences identified and approved of by the teacher and the National Curriculum, but not necessarily to achieve any practical results. As a result, it is easy for pupils to become alienated from the tasks set, for they lack the motivation that would be provided by writing with a real purpose for a real audience, for the teacher is no more than a simulated audience. Writing, too, can often become meaningless and routinized, something they have to do and over which they have little control.

Many teachers of English may wish to exempt written work in English lessons from these criticisms. Some hold that when pupils explore in writing their own experience and concerns they obtain personal benefits even though they are not addressing themselves to other persons or to practical tasks. This is certainly true for some pupils on some occasions, but much of the writing done in English does not support this account. There is much writing of stories that reproduce familiar fictional stereotypes, and even when the topic is a personal one it is often clear that pupils are covering paper merely in order to satisfy a teacher's demands, and not from a desire to throw light upon their experiences. Writing may be more often enjoyed in English than in other lessons, but many pupils nevertheless see this writing as irrelevant to the real business of living.

Teachers, faced with alienated conscripts, may give writing quite a different purpose even from that intended in the educational rhetoric, for it often serves as an important means of behavioural control in the classroom. Teachers know that when classes are made to settle down to written work they are usually quieter and can be more easily disciplined than when they are engaged in other learning activities. One reason for the success of writing is that it is a tangible and easily measured product:

> *Teacher:*   [to pupil on front row] . . . Four lines!
> [to his companion] . . . Three lines!

Such oblique comments are readily interpreted by pupils, and these remarks, made in a surprised and slightly sarcastic tone, had the immediate effect of silencing two chatterers. In our experience it is common for teachers to 'patrol' a classroom, noting how much writing certain pupils had completed as a way of judging how much work had been done. Under such circumstances, length of work becomes the indicator of effort and conformity. The emphasis on length is coupled with the view that if children are not continuously engaged in the physical process of writing, then they are probably wasting time. A fine example of this was when one teacher said: 'Come on. Some of you are staring out of the window and doing absolutely nothing.' The remark was made in a lesson in which the pupils had been asked to write down their thought on 'Miracles'.

In our research we also found that writing was frequently set as a punishment for misbehaviour. Lack of effort or bad behaviour in class were usually punished by keeping a pupil in class during breaks or lunchtimes and setting them written work to do, or by setting essays to be done for homework. In addition, essays were used as a punishment for many offences out of class, such as lateness or misbehaviour in corridors.

Thus writing has negative associations for pupils, in a way that other language activities do not:

1 Writing for many pupils is artificial because it is work that is unrelated to their needs and purposes as they perceive them.
2 Writing is hard work because in school one must do it continuously at times prescribed by the teacher.
3 Writing is a mechanism for exposing pupils who play about.
4 Writing is associated with punishment.

Our research suggested that for pupils, writing was often perceived as an onerous task, to be got out of the way as quickly as possible, as part of the whole process of 'getting through' the school day, and indeed the whole school system. There was very little positive commitment to written work, or enjoyment of it, among those pupils who were interviewed, particularly those designated of 'lower ability'. We may well see this as an additional reason why pupils may be unresponsive to the clues that teachers provide about the ground rules for writing. For there will be a whole cohort of pupils whose main aim is to get the right amount done with the minimum amount of effort.

But there may be even more subtle ways in which the writing done in schools relates to the wider social structure and serves to maintain existing social relations. It is this that we now explore.

The dominant public model of the purpose of education in the English educational system is one where learning is seen as primarily a liberating process for the individual. The model is curiously apolitical, overtly at least, despite the reforms of the late 1980s. It presupposes a society where individuals can live out their lives on a personal level, interacting with the polity only when they cast their vote, sign a petition or help the economy by becoming an engineer. Traditionally, 'politics' has been equated with 'party politics', and teachers have been exhorted to keep politics out of education, and party bias and propaganda out of the classroom. Only recently, in the acrid debate about the National Curriculum version of history, has there been an increasing awareness that the ordinary secondary curriculum is a political construct, that the way school knowledge is selected and taught can influence how pupils think, and that it is impossible to have a politically value-free curriculum. The history controversy has made us more aware of the idea that subject content is consciously or unconsciously selected to represent a particular ideological position, but as Harold Rosen (1984) has argued, we ought also to become aware that the carriers of content – the forms of writing that we are so familiar with in school – perform similar functions. At various levels they act to constrain pupils' behaviour and even their thinking.

First, the writing that we do always exists within a cultural and historical context that has shaped its conventions. Writing genres, therefore, reflect the dominant values and assumptions of the societies that produce them. Secondly, the form of writing, even when not closely related to its content, can have powerful effects on attitudes, beliefs and behaviour. We learn early on, for example, that our polite thank-you letter is sure to elicit another Christmas present from Auntie the following year. The letter form itself is an ancient convention, but variously moulded and modified by its cultural context. Today, we unthinkingly adopt one current manifestation, which carries with it a cargo of tacit meanings, as the way to say 'Thank you'.

We find it difficult to conceive of writing that is not within a particular genre, and we find it almost unthinkable to move out of the conventions we have been taught as the appropriate ones for the particular social situation we find ourselves in. We have an unconscious belief in various literary forms as immutable, even though such obvious ones as the novel or the poem are clearly the product of the interplay of cultural forces and subject to changes in conventions over the years. In the preceding chapters, we have discussed in some detail the main genres for school writing: the scientific report and the essay, for example. We have pointed out what teachers need to do in order to help their pupils to achieve competence in these forms, but we have also voiced criticism of those teachers who uncritically accept that there are only a limited number of genres available, one being suitable for all the written work associated with the subject that they teach.

We are concerned about this attitude because, as we have shown, it rests in part on a fundamental misconception of the nature of 'disciplined' thinking. But we are also inclined to reject it because it has serious implications for the development of critical thinking by pupils. To work always within the confines of conventional discourse models, usually those predominating in the academic areas of higher education, is to create certain restricting attitudes, assumptions and habits of thought in the minds of the pupils. First, it encourages uncritical conformity to existing arrangements; the process of teaching writing becomes simply a matter of making pupils conform to dominant genres. Such styles of writing are not seen as provisional, neither do they encourage the learner to integrate the knowledge at any depth into the frames that shape actions in everyday life. The writing process ceases to be creative and interactive, the genre no longer a facilitator in a state of flux and development but a rigid straitjacket to constrain the mind rather than liberate it. The writing can so easily become a parody of itself as pupils strive for a precocity of style that is not their own. The product is an abstracted affair, divorced from the real learning experiences of the child.

We see the adult equivalent of this in the unnecessary bureaucratic jargon of official reports, absurd 'legalese' and elsewhere. Adults conform to such genres from habit, but also from fear of being looked down upon, and from a lack of confidence in their ability to adapt available forms or to generate a voice of their own. While sometimes we may find the existing forms convenient and suitable, there is no doubt that at other times we keep within them because of social pressures, external or internalized.

The unquestioning adoption of such genres may have other implications as well. Our public adult writing conventions for transactional prose reflect an emphasis in our society in hiding personal involvement and experiences, of pretending that subjective attitudes and feelings are objective fact. They create documents that appear to have an independent life, separate from the personality of the author and independent of the processes that made up their production. We may thus tend to believe that the contents also represent some objective and thus more valid kind of knowledge or opinion. This process can be reversed, however, and a personalized genre used as a tool for manipulation, as in this report from a financial fund manager:

> Quite clearly I should have seen the writing on the wall (whilst it was still standing in fact!) and bought into Germany earlier and heavier. However, I have always been averse to buying things that have already risen and are 'flavour of the month' preferring to spend my time seeking out a recovery idea or an unresearched company. With hindsight I was probably trying to be too clever . . .

A few lines later the text switches suddenly to a quite different genre with sentences such as, 'Warrants are a geared exposure to a share.' What is the fund manager's intention in bringing together the two genres? Readers might like to consider how this is likely to affect clients' attitudes to the company. Is human frailty and the subjectivity of the enterprise being exposed, or are we intended to recognize that a competent and reflective person is at work, and thus gain confidence in the manager of the investments?

Pseudo-objectification of writing occurs in education at all levels. It is typical of the vast bulk of children's writing in school, particularly in subjects that strain to be scientific in approach. It is typical of the university thesis, and even apparent in educational journals where real teachers, pupils and researchers become abstracted ciphers discussed in tortuous prose in an attempt to create scientific credibility. The habit of thought which the unquestioning acceptance of such writing creates is the notion of free-standing objectivity of observations and theories, of a truth with an independent existence, untainted by personal preferences and perspectives, free from political ideology. We wish to argue here that this is an impossible ideal and that, far from providing a vehicle for the truth, teachers' emphasis on confining pupils' writing within rigid genres, especially those we have just discussed above, is itself an ideological activity. It is part of processes operating at the level of the classroom that ultimately support the wider social structure and power relationships of our society.

For such an approach to writing socializes children into certain attitudes to both the nature of knowledge and the nature of society. They learn that conforming and fitting into structures and systems is the way to get on in school. They also learn that what is, is. They develop a particular conception of the nature of knowledge, of social and political relationships – that such things have deep unchanging rules within which there is room for a little manoeuvre, but not much. In many textbooks, the provisional nature of knowledge is not revealed in the authoritative accounts couched in the language of absolute truth, rather than tentativeness, fallibility and essential humanity. And now, in making this point, we have reached a position similar to that which ended our discussion of the nature of disciplined thinking, and again leave further comments on the implications of this analysis to the final section of the chapter.

Some speculations: ground rules and social class

It seems most likely that children's ability in learning and writing is a product of complex environmental influences both from home and school, and that much of their learning in this area is not the product of conscious and directed teaching, but is accumulated as various experiences provide interpretive frameworks and ground rules for communication – cognitive and communicative habits that lead to varying degrees of success or failure in the system. There is, however, considerable evidence to suggest that life chances do not operate in an entirely random way, and many writers have pointed to a discernible social class pattern in the distribution of access to ground rules. Our own research has not systematically explored the link, as we chose instead to unravel some of the complexities of the way the rules operate in the classroom. However, it is worth recording here what some of the evidence suggests, as it once again points up the relationship between habits of thought and writing and the maintenance of power relationships in society.

As far as writing is concerned, Moffett (1968) is one of a number of educationalists to hint at a social class connection in relation to cognitive and communicative skills. He begins by commenting on the way 'underdeveloped' teenage writers fail to display a mastery of certain ground rules:

> Whether they are writing stories or ideas, children overcondense at first and only later become able to elaborate and expand. But many underdeveloped high school students have the same limitations; they write only synopses and one can feel their reluctance to leave the haven of narrative. (Moffett, 1968, p. 133)

Writing at the time when Bernstein's theories of language codes had gained widespread recognition, Moffett doubted that this phenomenon was due simply to psychological immaturity. He went on to suggest that it could be explained by applying Bernstein's theory that different language patterns and habits of thought are the result of different social relations and social control techniques in the working- and middle-classes.

By the 1970s, much more sociological evidence was emerging that lends support to the concepts of ground rules and interpretive schemata which we have elaborated, and which presented a more sophisticated account of the effect of social class on communicative habits. By 1971, Bernstein had clarified his earlier ideas and established that he was talking about class differences in the use of ground rules rather than using a simplistic notion of 'arrested' development due to language deprivation (a misinterpretation of Bernstein that had wide currency during the 1960s). He even used the term 'ground rules' in some of his writing. Here, for example, he comments on the reasons for middle-class children's more elaborate and, therefore, more successful verbal performances in interviews:

> I suggest that what we are witnessing are differences in the ground rules the children are using to generate their meanings and so their speech. . . . One group of children, through their initial socialisation, are applying one set of ground rules, and another group of children are applying a different set.

And in a footnote, he adds:

> Ground rules lie behind manifest behaviour in ways similar to those in which grammatical rules lie behind speech. Elaborated and restricted codes from this perspective have their basis in different ground rules. (Bernstein, 1971b, p. 254)

Others like Keddie (1971) and Tough (1977) reported similar findings as children grappled with the ground rules for teacher–pupil interaction in the classroom and in interviews. But it is only the French sociologist Bourdieu (1974) who has focused on these issues specifically in relation to writing.

Bourdieu relates the different success rates of working- and middle-class children in the French Literature Baccalaureate examination to the fact that working-class children lack what he calls 'cultural capital'. This consists of underlying knowledge of nuances of manners and style, which are necessary for school success, but which are not explicitly taught by the school. Instead, he argues, such cultural capital is transmitted to middle-class children by their families during early socialization. To understand what is taught and to write effectively, children have to crack the communication 'code' that operates in the classroom. Only children who possess the appropriate styles of thought and presentation can do so.

Bourdieu defines cultural capital as 'style', but this is a term that needs careful clarification, as it refers to much more than the conventional stylistic skills that we associate with the fluent essay writer. What Bourdieu is suggesting is that *cognitive* styles are part of cultural capital as well. The way in which all academic knowledge is framed, and the underlying assumptions that are made by teachers and examiners when setting academic tasks must also be taken into account (q.v. the concept of 'critical thinking' that was discussed earlier). The 'code' provided by cultural capital is thus a set of interpretive frameworks that give middle-class children an advantage in understanding the implicit demands being made of them in the classroom, in terms of both content and style of writing.

Those students who fall 'naturally' into providing types of answer and styles of writing – and ways of organizing content – that are consonant with middle-class examiners' cultural background and expectations are likely to be those students who have been socialized within a similar cultural milieu and whose work appears stylish and effortlessly fluent while displaying obvious talent. Bourdieu goes on to comment on the contrast between this kind of writing and the more forced and clumsier work of those unfortunates who had to work hard in school to identify and practise the appropriate rules because they came from a background that did not provide them.

Bourdieu argues that schools help to perpetuate inequality by a process of simple neglect, which automatically tends to lead to the failure of those who came to school without the necessary ground rules:

> To penalise the underprivileged and favour the most privileged, the school has only to neglect, in its teaching methods and techniques and in its criteria for making academic judgements, to take into account the cultural inequalities between children of different social classes. (Bourdieu, 1974, pp. 37–8)

Even if we have reservations about the crude social class correlations that sociologists attempt to draw, they do nevertheless draw our attention to the influence of the wider socio-cultural settings that influence the thinking styles of our pupils. As teachers, we are then confronted with the problem of how we should alter our teaching styles in the light of this knowledge, and what we can really achieve by so doing.

The status of the ground rules

How inflexible are the tacit expectations and social practices that we are calling ground rules? Certainly, some are deeply embedded both in our schooling and in our lives outside school. It is difficult to imagine a public educational system that does not mainly rest upon 'what if?' modes of thought and does not at times shape young people's thinking via the formalized tasks we have called 'disembedded logic'. On the other hand, there are other ground rules that are far less inflexible, including the conventions of writing in various genres. Harold Rosen has pointed out that these conventions constrain not merely the use of words but the meanings that can be expressed: the ground rules of writing are implicitly ways of shaping the world that their users live in.

> Millions of notebooks, examination papers, and 'essays' are crammed with words which are in essence no more than transcriptions, the forced labour of submission. (Rosen, 1984)

For example, the typical school science report focuses attention upon abstract physical processes, and prevents any attention being given to the social and environmental implications of putting this knowledge to use. Thus the ground rules of the science report help to define the boundaries of science in a way that may obscure crucially important human aspects of scientific knowledge. Similarly, as has been pointed out in an earlier chapter, much writing in English lessons limits the range of topics that can appropriately be addressed, preferring personal relationships to topics of wider import.

Of course, the conventions that govern language use cannot be ignored. Wherever we learn to talk and write, in whatever context and for whatever purpose, we do so in terms of existing ways of using language and (inevitably) of existing ways of understanding our experiences. But these conventions are not monolithic nor unchanging. Rosen (1984) writes:

> The legitimised forms of language are constantly being eroded and undermined – and not just by children. . . . Writing is a site of conflict and ferocious play goes on within its boundaries. Old forms die out and new ones appear, others are in a state of flux.

He cites the changing patterns of book dedications and the variety of modes in which a philosophical work can be couched. He might equally have pointed to the changing styles chosen by political candidates in the documents that come through our letter boxes before an election. To represent the ground rules of writing as immutable is simply to mislead. But this is not to imply that each one of us has a unique voice to speak with, irrespective of the written and spoken genres we hear about us. Those writers who do achieve a personal voice do so out of a prolonged and critical engagement with the genres that have been available in their social milieu: there is no easy route. But Rosen is right to insist that we should support and encourage such a critical engagement, even for those young people who are never likely to produce 'original' writing. Critical awareness of writing genres can be closely linked with critical awareness of the meanings our culture makes available.

The matter is complicated by the fact that some of these conventions are deeply involved in the ways in which power is exerted over us in everyday life. For example, if we wish to be considered for a job it behooves us to write an application in a style that our potential employers will approve. If we wish to complain to an official, our letter is more likely to be read attentively if we advance arguments in a style that will persuade the reader that our views should be listened to. If we want a newspaper to publish a letter, we have to attend to the probable expectations of the editor and the readers. In such situations as these we have a choice: we may judge that self-censorship will be justified by the outcome, or we may ignore other people's expectations and damn the consequences. The point we are making is that teachers should not tell young people that they should submit, but should make them sufficiently aware both of the conventions, including the appropriate ground rules, and of the likely cost of ignoring them. In the end, it is the individual who needs to be in a position to choose whether to conform or rebel. If we pretend that ground rules do not exist, we mislead our pupils; if we tell them that ground rules are to be obeyed unquestioningly, we betray them at a deeper level. It should be kept in mind throughout the later section of this chapter in which we discuss ways of increasing pupils' awareness of ground rules that the awareness we have in mind is a critical one.

Making ground rules visible to pupils

We have repeatedly noted throughout this book that most teachers adopt an 'intuitive' model of language teaching across the curriculum. By this we mean that the rules of the writing game are largely left unspoken, and it is assumed that learners will gradually absorb what they need to know. By contrast, those subject teachers who do feel that specific writing skills need to be taught, often attempt to do so by baldly stating what is required rather than by integrating the teaching of writing into the lesson. Many teachers, we found, believed in the concept of 'natural flair' and thought that teachers need not – in fact, could not – systematically teach the required writing competences. Alongside this went the view shared by most progressive teachers that old-fashioned didactic teaching methods were no way to teach writing.

Basil Bernstein (1975) made a distinction between what he called 'visible' and 'invisible pedagogy'. Visible pedagogy referred to teaching that spelt out clearly to pupils what was expected of them, giving them little or no opportunity to join in the thinking or to choose for themselves. Invisible pedagogy referred to 'progressive' methods of teaching in which pupils were given a considerable amount of choice in what they did and how they did it. Bernstein's point was that whatever the teaching style it would be the teacher who controlled the ground rules, so that the pupils who already knew the rules – who looked at the picture books rather than playing with sand all day – would be perceived from the first to be academically promising (Sharp and Green, 1975). It seemed probable that children from professional families would be more likely to choose the activities that teachers approve of, so that, according to Bernstein's reasoning, invisible pedagogy would work to the disadvantage of working-class children, however excellent the intentions of the liberal-minded teachers who practise such teaching methods.

The outcome of this line of thought should not be a return to more authoritarian teaching. Teachers of all subjects must help their pupils to develop appropriate strategies for the writing needed in their subject. Such teaching should be generated from the content needs of particular lessons, and should be part of a wider practice of revealing the ground rules of cognition and communication to pupils. The overall intention would thus be to enable pupils to reflect critically on the requirements for particular kinds of writing and their own strategies in seeking to meet them. It is not enough, however, to leave those readers who are practising teachers with advice in such general terms, so the remainder of this section is devoted to practical suggestions about how this might be done in lessons.

In an earlier chapter, we wrote that teachers should think more precisely about the nature of the tasks they set, because some of the difficulties their pupils face are created there and then in the classroom. Pierre Bourdieu (1974) has said that 'Teachers assume that they already share a common language and set of values with their pupils', and argues that this creates a major barrier for the many pupils – perhaps the majority – who do not do so. Because teachers control the rules of the game in their classrooms, those pupils who are unaware that they are playing by different rules will lose. Pupils' success in school depends in part upon their ability to recognize certain aspects of lessons as salient: those who miss the teacher's cues will appear to be uncooperative or stupid. What they say and write will appear to be irrelevant and irrational; for any pupil whose manner is aggressive, this irrelevance may even be construed as insolence by any teacher who is insecure.

It is thus very important that all teachers should be as aware as possible of the ground rules that they are tacitly operating and do their best to interpret and explain them to pupils. However, because ground rules are a universal part of social life, making them explicit will not make them disappear, however sensitive and helpful the teacher is. Explanations may not be of much help to some pupils for whom they are likely to prove as incomprehensible as the invisible rules themselves. Methods are needed that will enable these pupils gradually to understand what is required: some of these are suggested below. We shall go on later in the chapter to consider whether some ground rules should be challenged, perhaps by teachers and pupils together.

Making the ground rules explicit

After a few years of teaching, it is easy for any teacher to have so well-established a picture of 'the right kind of writing for my subject' that he or she forgets that it needs to be made available to pupils. Indeed, teachers of most subjects expect a range of different styles of discourse for different purposes, but do not always succeed in making these changes clear to their pupils. An explanation of what is required – which most good teachers undertake in any case – is essential when work of a new kind is set, but explanation alone is unlikely to be enough. It may only be when pupils have made some attempt at the task that explanations will be of any use to them. When younger pupils produce writing that is absurdly inappropriate, it is important not to mock them, or interpret their error as disobedience. Their misunderstanding may need to be dealt with either individually, or – if it can be done tactfully – as an example to others in the class. For an experienced teacher, the error will not appear as an absurdity but as evidence that ground rules have not been grasped. Moreover, it may be necessary to return on more than one occasion to the same requirements. Though a busy teacher, aware of the pressure of a syllabus, may not wish to devote much time to helping pupils to grasp what kind of writing is required, this may prevent future failures and conflicts that would be much more time-consuming.

In Chapter 1 we mentioned a biology teacher who showed pupils a film urging young people to take good care of their teeth, and then asked them to 'write it up' for homework. The writing that resulted was a confused amalgam of styles, because the pupils were unclear whether they were to reproduce the persuasive style of the film, or to discuss the issues abstractly, or to produce a 'factual summary' in the style often required in science reports. The pupils could not ask the teacher because they were quite unaware of the dilemma that was to mar their work. A few minutes discussion of possible ways of tackling the task, including some alternative ways of phrasing, could have helped to clear the confusion. (It is not at all obvious to most 15-year-olds that 'We all ought to look after our teeth' belongs in a different universe of discourse from 'Caries is a disease of the teeth'.) It is worth noticing that this particular misunderstanding did not in the least depend upon whether or not the pupils understood the content. Nor could the problem have been dealt with beforehand, perhaps in English lessons, for it had been created there and then in the biology lesson.

Purposes of teaching the ground rules

Preparatory discussion of written work will have several related purposes. In the first place, the pupils need to be clear about the content and purpose of the writing to be done. Much school writing is done to order without the pupils having an opportunity to formulate for themselves what its purposes are. In secondary schools, there is much copying of notes from blackboards or from dictation, much mechanical summarizing of material from lessons or from textbooks, and even (for some pupils) much sentence-completion by writing a word in a slot. These activities will certainly not help young people to learn to control their own writing. For example, less able pupils do not always grasp that the purpose of writing is to increase their understanding and not merely to cover a page with handwriting. If we do not treat learners as competent to understand the purposes of writing, we must not be surprised when they fail to grasp the ground rules and produce work that is both feeble and inappropriate.

It will help them to understand what is required if they have already been involved in thinking about the topic, rather than merely listening to the teacher. In this we are including generating ideas, asking questions, formulating guesses and hypotheses, and reorganizing material for other purposes. (In Chapter 2 we mentioned how pupils who were interviewed about science reports they had written often showed that they had not understood the purpose of the practical work they were describing, or its relationship to the scientific principles involved.) This work on the content of the lessons will help them to grasp the ground rules that govern what their teacher will think relevant ideas and information, and will make links between what they already know and the new ways of thinking that are being presented in the lesson.

The point we are making is that if pupils have been able to formulate the aims of the writing in their own terms, they will be more able to adopt the framework of ground rules required by the discipline in question. As Rosen (1967) and others have pointed out, a pupil who does not really understand the purpose of the writing often takes refuge in a desperate attempt to mimic the standard style of the subject, stringing technical phrases together in a way that demonstrates nothing but panic-stricken incomprehension. Most of our readers will upon occasion have received writing like this: it is the mark of those who are half aware that they have entirely failed to grasp the ground rules.

But pupils will need to understand not only the ground rules that govern the choice of content, they will also need help in finding a structure for the piece, and in choosing an appropriate style and tone. This is where the discussion of examples is essential: it would be valuable if all secondary pupils were aware of the choices they must make between alternative modes of discourse, rather than doing so by intuition alone, which may serve some well but leave many blind. Perhaps it is the task of the English teacher to introduce this way of thinking about writing, and discuss it at length, but every teacher should be reinforcing this awareness, because many of the choices depend on considerations that are specific to particular subjects and even to particular occasions. For example, it is only the history teacher who can help his or her pupils to sort out whether on a particular occasion what is wanted is a summary of information, an evaluation and comparison of alternative sources, a reconstruction of the experience of persons living in the past, or an evaluative analysis of the work of a prominent figure or group. Each of these implies not only different content but also a different mode of discourse, including choices of structure, style and tone. There seems every reason why history teachers should help pupils to be aware of this range of discourses, and why science teachers should take similar responsibility for the range of discourses that their work requires. Ground rules are the responsibility of every teacher.

Methods of teaching ground rules

Preparation for an unfamiliar writing task should always include the discussion of examples, both those in which the task is well done and those where it is not, though the latter should if possible not be taken from the class in question. For example, a history teacher might make a collection of examples of pupils' attempts (more and less successful) at each of the four discourse modes mentioned in the previous paragraph, and use these on appropriate occasions as the basis for discussing what is expected. It is much harder to learn from abstractions than from examples: even adults can often make use of theoretical explanations only when they have half grasped the point in a less abstract way.

There is much to be said for finding out what the pupils *think* will be required, because it is often inappropriate ground rules brought from elsewhere that need to be dealt with. One way of doing this would be to give out copies of a piece of written work from a former pupil who had attempted a similar task, and to ask the class to discuss – perhaps in groups – in what ways it was appropriate or inappropriate. Their reports on their discussions would throw a great deal of light on their current conceptions of what was expected and therefore provide an excellent basis for increasing their awareness of ground rules. Dixon (1988) recommends that genres should be 'taught in a dialogue ... that organises, clarifies and draws lessons from a joint enquiry by students'.

The pupils' own writing will similarly throw light upon what they expect, if teachers read them as evidence of their current ground rules rather than simply for evaluation. How written work is 'marked' is also of crucial importance. In Chapter 2 we mentioned a teacher who had underlined 'or else' in a pupil's science report. The red underlining, the question-mark and the 'unsatisfactory' in the margin, are alike useless as feedback to the pupil who has not yet grasped the ground rules that apply, for they express disapproval but do not convey what is being disapproved of. Pupils are unlikely to learn from their failures unless the teacher can steal a moment or two to talk individually about what was inappropriate or misconceived in a piece of writing that a pupil has done. We made a similar point in Chapter 3 about the two pupils who copied out lengthy passages about the Bridgewater Canal. They had not grasped the ground rules that guide the sifting, selection and reinterpreting of information in history and social studies, and only came to understand why mechanical copying was irrelevant after the teacher had discussed the purpose of the work with the two of them. If the teacher had not done this, two pupils would have been left with a sense that they 'couldn't do history', but without any means of remedying this.

Of course, it is more economical if such discussion can be carried out with a whole class, and it is not impossible to do this, if tactful use is made of written work that has already been done. The purpose is to make each pupil a critical reader of his or her own work, and one way of doing this with some classes may be to give them an opportunity to read one another's work and discuss it in the privacy of a small group of peers. We are suggesting that the pupils should work together to identify which parts of the writing seem not to meet what they think appropriate, and to discuss why this is so. In doing so, they will have to explore the ground rules that members of the group are currently using. Such a lesson can end with the teacher taking one or two positive examples and explaining why they meet with his or her approval. There would seem to be opportunities for teachers of English to collaborate with colleagues who teach another subject in doing work of this kind.

Any of these kinds of discussion is likely to improve pupils' written work. Some teachers may think these proposals intolerable when the weight of syllabus content is considered, but they should realize that pupils who constantly find their written work being rejected and criticized without being able to understand why are likely to stop trying to do well, and join the ranks of the disaffected and badly behaved. It is not by any means obvious that time spent in avoiding this is time wasted.

Critical rather than prescriptive teaching

There may be a danger that ground rules will be ascribed a more permanent and explicit status than they deserve. Some writers have identified speech and writing 'genres' essential for success in schools and have proposed that they should be taught to pupils. However, in our view, the use of the concept 'genre' carries dangers with it. In Chapter 1, we quoted from a paper by Christie (1985) a passage in which she argued that 'those who fail in schools are those who fail to master the genres of schooling', and went on to describe genres as 'ways . . . of dealing with experience'. This seems on the face of it consonant with the view of ground rules that we have presented, except in so far as 'genre' includes a more limited range than 'ground rules'.

There are elements in Christie's position that give us pause. As she herself indicates, at the centre of a genre is a 'way of meaning', that is, a way of understanding the world. Any adult must have a repertoire of 'ways of meaning', including some derived from schooling and others that come from that person's work, family or leisure interests. Those from schooling – frameworks of understanding, such as history or physics – have been selected because they are held to play a particularly important place in the culture (or cultures) of our time and place. Our discussion of ground rules has suggested that schools also have other kinds of requirements that pupils have to meet in order to succeed, though it seems unlikely that most of these can appropriately be called 'genres'.

A disadvantage of thinking about ways of meaning in terms of 'genre', however, is that 'genre' carries with it implications that refer to the surface structures of linguistic behaviour. That is, a genre is associated with a 'register', a set of linguistic forms and practices, especially preferred vocabulary and grammar. Christie refers, for example, to identifying a genre by 'uncovering a schematic structure', and elsewhere uses the phrase 'learning how to manipulate the various linguistic items'. Is this really what we mean by 'genre'? It is true that by manipulating linguistic items we enter into communication with others in ways that exemplify our mastery or otherwise of ground rules or of genres, but the centre of the genre is the 'way of meaning', not the linguistic items. The language of a school subject is often used by pupils in ways that precisely demonstrate their *failure* to grasp the ground rules of the genre. Freadman (1988) uses Wittgenstein's game metaphor to demonstrate that it is the occasion or 'place' of an utterance, rather than an amalgam of linguistic features, that constitutes its genre.

To object to phrases taken out of context from Christie's paper may seem like splitting hairs; however, the danger of focusing upon the surface features of genres rather than upon their meanings is that it may, perhaps quite unintentionally, transmit dangerous messages about how students should be made aware of them. Dixon (1988) warns Christie against an 'exclusive interest in easily observable formal changes', and adds 'Without new practices in the classroom culture, I see little hope for changes in most students' writing – the shifts we perceive will lie on the rhetorical surface.' Teaching the surface forms of genres may prove self-defeating.

Even though Christie's line of thought bears a close resemblance to the arguments we have used here, we do not think that we are dealing with anything so clearly defined as genres. Even the terms 'ground rules' will be misleading if they suggest a finite number of procedures that can be exhaustively defined and taught. There is a danger that some teachers might specify the requirements (for a history essay, for example) in terms which give them the force of law, thus intolerably constraining their pupils' writings. Though we use the term 'rules', we do not see them as similar to the binding rules of a club, for example, but rather as a description of patterns of behaviour that can be observed, but which are open to change and reinterpretation. They are thus a topic for collaborative investigation rather than authoritative statement.

It is probably impossible to spell out fully the processes by which a competent writer begins to generate an overall plan by trying out sub-plans, and at the same time monitors the developing text both from the point of view of his or her half-formulated intentions and from a sense of the needs of potential readers. In such a complex activity as writing, there will always be a considerable element of intuitive judgement, of learning by doing. In our attempt to help pupils to deal with quasi-invisible requirements, we must not fall into the trap of hyper-rationalism: well-intentioned attempts to control everything all too often produce unintended results. Communication in natural language, whether written or spoken, seldom has the unambiguous clarity that mathematicians aspire to. (Do they achieve it?) We manage to communicate through a series of approximations: we negotiate and repair; we agree on a form of words and sort out their meaning later. This is why we recommend that teachers discuss ground rules with their pupils not once but briefly on many occasions.

We are clear that ground rules can never be fully specified, for they change subtly with each purpose and context. In Chapter 1, we found it more appropriate to present them through examples than through definitions. As we showed in Chapter 4, some attempts by examining boards to spell out in detail what writing they require has led to caricatures that are as disabling to pupils as the more open tasks that they replaced. Indeed, some ground rules may disadvantage pupils just as effectively when they are explicit as when they are concealed. Our hope, however, is that ground rules can be made less powerful by being deconstructed.

If the writing tasks set in schools cannot be understood unless the pupil is acquainted with ground rules, do not those ground rules need to be interpreted by a second order of meta-ground rules, and those by further rules *ad infinitum*? As Wittgenstein made clear, in the last analysis we learn to use the meanings available in a group by sharing in the activities of that group; our interest in ground rules is not intended to deny this. Edwards and Mercer (1987) have demonstrated some of the procedures by which teachers in primary schools may tacitly induct their pupils into some of the interpretive frameworks needed in science, social studies and elsewhere in the curriculum. We accept the validity of their account, and wish to add to it only that the pupils will be trapped by these frames rather than enabled unless they have the opportunity to reflect critically on them. We believe that young people's ability to make use of their school experiences will be enhanced if tacit meanings are made explicit, and their acceptability criticized.

References

Barnes, D. and Seed, J. (1984). Seals of approval: An analysis of English examinations. In Goodson, I. F. and Ball, S. (eds), *Defining the Curriculum*. London: Falmer Press, 263–98.

Barnes, D., Barnes, D. and Clarke, S. (1984). *Versions of English*. London: Heinemann Educational.

Bereiter, C. and Scardamalia, S. (1982). From conversation to composition: The role of instruction in a developmental process. In Glaser, R. (ed.), *Advances in Instructional Psychology*. London: Lawrence Erlbaum Associates, 1–64.

Bernstein, B. (1971a). On the classification and framing of educational knowledge. In Young, M. F. D. (ed.), *Knowledge and Control*. London: Collier-Macmillan, 47–69.

Bernstein, B. (1971b). *Class, Codes and Control* Vol. 1. London: Routledge and Kegan Paul.

Bernstein, B. (1971c). A socio-linguistic approach to socialisation. In Young, M. F. D. (ed.), *Knowledge and Control*. London: Collier-Macmillan.

Bernstein, B. (1975). Class and pedagogies: Visible and invisible. Paris: Organisation for Economic Co-operation and Development.

Booth, M., Culpin, C. and Macintosh, H. (1987). *Teaching GCSE history*. London: Hodder and Stoughton.

Bourdieu, P. (1974). The school as a conservative force: Scholastic and cultural inequalities. In Eggleston, J. (ed.), *Contemporary Research in the Sociology of Education*. London: Methuen, 32–46.

Britton, J. N., Burgess, T., Martin, N., McLeod, A. and Rosen, H. (1975). *The Development of Writing Abilities*. London: Macmillan.

Britton, J. N., with Barrs, M. and Burgess, T. (1979). No, no, Jeanette: A reply to Jeanette Williams' critique of the Schools Council Writing Research Project. *Language for Learning* 1 (1), 23–41.

Brookfield, S. (1987). *Developing Critical Thinkers*. Milton Keynes: Open University Press.

Central Advisory Council for Education (England) (1963). *Half Our Future*. London: HMSO.

Christie, F. (1985). Language and schooling. In Tchudi, S. (ed.), *Language, Schooling and Society*. Portsmouth, NH: Boynton-Cook, 21–40.

Cooper, B. (1976). *Bernstein's Codes: A Classroom Study*. Brighton: University of Sussex Education Area Occasional Paper, No. 6.

Department of Education and Science (1975). *A Language for Life* (The Bullock Report). London: HMSO.

Dixon, J. (1988). The question of genres. In Reid, I. (ed.), *The Place of Genre in Learning: Current Debates*. Geelong: Deakin University, 9–21.

Donaldson, M. (1978). *Children's Minds*. London: Fontana/Croom Helm.

Edwards, A. D. (1974). *Language in Culture and Class*. London: Heinemann.

Edwards, D. and Mercer, N. (1987). *Common Knowledge*. London: Methuen.

Freadman, A. (1988). Anyone for tennis? In Reid, I. (ed.), *The Place of Genre in Learning: Current Debates*. Geelong: Deakin University, 91–124.

Goodson, I. (1988). *The Making of Curriculum: Collected Essays*. Lewes: Falmer Press.

Hawkins, P. R. (1969). Social class, the nominal group, and reference. In Bernstein, B. (ed.), *Class, Codes and Control* Vol. 2. London: Routledge and Kegan Paul, 81–92.

Hirst, P. H. (1974). *Knowledge and the Curriculum*. London: Routledge and Kegan Paul.

Hirst, P. H. and Peters, R. S. (1970). *The Logic of Education*. London: Routledge and Kegan Paul.

Hull, R. (1985). *The Language Gap: How Classroom Dialogue Fails*. London: Methuen.

Keddie, N. (1971). Classroom knowledge. In Young, M. F. D. (ed.), *Knowledge and Control*. London: Collier-Macmillan, 133–60.

Kuhn, T. S. (1970). *The Structure of Scientific Revolutions*, 2nd edn. Chicago: University of Chicago Press.

Medway, P. (1980). *Finding a Language: Autonomy and Learning in School*. London: Writers and Readers Publishing Cooperative.

Medway, P. (1986a). What counts as English: Selections from language and reading in a school subject at the twelve year old level. Unpublished Ph.D. thesis, University of Leeds.

Medway, P. (1986b). What gets written about: Selections from real and imaginary worlds in school writing assignments. In Wilkinson, A. (ed.) *The Writing of Writing*. Milton Keynes: Open University Press, 29–39.

Medway, P. (1988). The student's world and the world of English. *English in Education* 22(2), 26–35.

Miller, C. M. and Parlett, M. (1976). Cue-consciousness. In Hammersley, M. and Woods, P. (eds), *The Process of Schooling*. London: Routledge and Kegan Paul, 143–9.

Moffett, J. (1968). *Teaching the Universe of Discourse*. New York: Houghton Mifflin.

Munby, H. and Russell, T. L. (1983). A common curriculum for the natural sciences. In *Individual Differences and the Common Curriculum 1983*. Chicago: National Society for the Study of Education, 160–85.

Peel, E. A. (1971). *The Nature of Adolescent Judgment*. London: Staples.

Postman, N. and Weingartner, C. (1969). *Teaching as a Subversive Activity*. New York: Delacorte Press.

Richards, J. (1978). *Classroom Language: What Sort?*. London: Allen and Unwin.

Rosen, H. (1967). The language of textbooks. In Cashdan, A. and Grugeon, E. (eds), *Language and Education*. London: Routledge and Kegan Paul, 119–25.

Rosen, H. (1972). *Language and Class: A Critical Look at the Theories of Basil Bernstein*. Bristol: Falling Wall Press.

Rosen, H. (1984). The politics of writing (unpublished lecture).

Russell, J. (1982). Propositional attitudes. In Beveridge, M. (ed.), *Children Thinking through Language*. London: Edward Arnold, 75–98.

Sharp, R. and Green, A. (1975). *Education and Social Control*. London: Routledge and Kegan Paul.

Shemilt, D. (1984). Empathy in history and the classroom. In Dickinson, A. K. *et al.* (eds), *Learning History*. London: Heinemann, 39–84.

Southern Regional Examinations Board (1986). *Empathy in History: From Definition to Assessment*. Southampton: SREB.

Spencer, E. (1983). *Writing Matters across the Curriculum*. London: Hodder and Stoughton.

Sutton, C. (ed.) (1981). *Communicating in the Classroom*. London: Hodder and Stoughton.

Tough, J. (1977). *The Development of Meaning: A Study of Children's Use of Language*. London: Allen and Unwin.

Wade, B. and Wood, A. (1979). Assessing writing in science. *Language for Learning* 1 (3), 131–8.

Williams, J. T. (1977). *Learning to Write or Writing to Learn*. Windsor: NFER.

Williams, M. (ed.) (1981). *Language, Teaching and Learning: 2 Geography*. London: Ward Lock.

Index